German 20th Century Poetry

The German Library: Volume 69

Volkmar Sander, General Editor

GERMAN
20TH CENTURY
POETRY

Edited by Reinhold Grimm
and Irmgard Hunt

CONTINUUM
NEW YORK · LONDON

2001

The Continuum International Publishing Group Inc
370 Lexington Avenue, New York, NY 10017

The Continuum International Publishing Group Ltd
The Tower Building, 11 York Road, London SE1 7NX

The German Library is published
in cooperation with Deutsches Haus, New York University.
This volume has been supported by Inter Nationes, and a grant
from the funds of Stifterverband für die Deutsche Wissenschaft.

Printed in the United States of America

Library of Congress Cataloging-in-Publication Data

German 20th century poetry / edited by Reinhold Grimm
and Irmgard Hunt.
         p.   cm. — (The German library ; v. 69)
    English and German.
    Includes index.
    ISBN 0-8264-1311-0 (alk. paper) — ISBN 0-8264-1312-9
(pbk. : alk. paper)
       1. German poetry—20th century—Translations into English.
 I. Title: German twentieth century poetry.   II. Grimm, Reinhold, 1931– .
    III. Hunt, Irmgard Elsner, 1944–   .   IV. Series.
    PT1160.E5 G37   2001
    831'.9108—dc21

                                                                00-052346

Acknowledgments will be found on page 271,
which constitutes an extension of the copyright page.

Contents

Contents · *vii*

Contents · ix

x · Contents

Prefatory Note

Embarras de richesses, an "embarrassing overabundance"—
this is perhaps the best way of characterizing the lyrical and
balladic output of the German-speaking countries, Germany her-
self and Austria in particular, over the past one hundred years. Be-
ginning with Hugo von Hofmannsthal, Stefan George, Rainer
Maria Rilke, and the balladeer Frank Wedekind, around that
proverbial turn of the century, 1900; continuing with Georg Trakl,
Georg Heym, the early Gottfried Benn, and so many others,
through that near equally proverbial expressionistic decade from
1910 to 1920 and, further, through the so-called roaring twenties,
which saw, most notably, the spectacular rise of the young Bertolt
Brecht; and, finally, reaching yet another peak, both quantitatively
and qualitatively, after World War II, with poets such as Paul Celan
and Ingeborg Bachmann, Karl Krolow and Hans Magnus Enzens-
berger: the 20th century does, indeed, constitute an era of great
and lasting German poetry comparable only to the poetic achieve-
ments of the age of Goethe and his Romantic followers from,
roughly, two hundred years ago. To document, even remotely, so
impressive a wealth of lyrics and ballads to everyone's satisfaction
proves to be all but impossible.

Luckily, a couple of the most eminent poets of this rich period
are already represented—or will be as it is planned—in respective
volumes of The German Library: to wit, Rilke (cf. Rainer Maria
Rilke, *Prose and Poetry,* ed. Egon Schwarz, foreword by Howard
Nemerov [German Library vol. 70]), Benn (cf. Gottfried Benn, *Prose
Essays Poems,* ed. Volkmar Sander, foreword by E. B. Ashton [Ger-

man Library vol. 73]), and the 1999 Nobel Prize winner Grass (cf. Günter Grass, *Cat and Mouse and Other Writings,* ed. A. Leslie Willson, foreword by John Irving [German Library vol. 93]); also, a volume of Brecht's poetry and prose (edited by Reinhold Grimm, with the collaboration of Caroline Molina y Vedia) is being prepared for publication. In addition, there exist two anthologies (cf. Wilhelm Busch and others, *German Satirical Writings,* ed. Dieter P. Lotze and Volkmar Sander, foreword by John Simon [German Library vol. 50] and *German Songs: Popular, Political, Folk, and Religious,* ed. Inke Pinkert-Sältzer [German Library vol. 53]), which contain poems from, and relevant to, our epoch; the former includes texts by Christian Morgenstern, Kurt Tucholsky, and Erich Kästner, the latter, "Songs of the Workers' Movement," "Anti-Fascist Songs," and "Songs of East and West Germany" (prominently featuring, needless to say, the *Liedermacher* [literally "songmakers"] who emerged in the late 1960s, Wolf Biermann being the finest and most widely known exponent). No examples of the writers that figure in these anthologies appear in the present selection, whereas in view of their authors' importance, a few verses by Rilke and Benn, Brecht and Grass, have been inserted for the sake of completeness and continuity.

It may be remembered that, more than forty years ago, the renowned German scholar Hugo Friedrich, a specialist in Romance letters, brought out a slim though weighty volume entitled *Die Struktur der modernen Lyrik* (The structure of modern poetry) which was an immediate and smashing success; since 1956, its year of publication, it has seen over a dozen editions, and been translated into several languages. In this seminal work, Friedrich claimed that modern poetry—truly modern poetry, that is—must be viewed as a basically French phenomenon: a development he traced, starting with Charles Baudelaire, to the verse of Arthur Rimbaud and Stéphane Mallarmé especially, whence it was said to have extended, during the 20th century, not only in France but also beyond, and to have influenced the Romance literatures—above all, those of Italy and Spain—in general. Contemporary poetry written in English received rather short shrift while that composed in German was treated almost marginally. A mere and meager threesome of poets from Germany (namely, Benn, Krolow, and Marie Luise Kaschnitz) and none from Austria or Switzerland were included in the vast florilegium of pertinent examples Friedrich appended to his authoritative disquisition; even George or the Austrians von Hofmannsthal, Rilke, and Trakl were conspicuously absent. However, this lopsided view and its concomitant evaluation have definitely changed in the meantime, and fairly early and drastically at that. No less a worthy than Hans Magnus Enzensberger, who, with his sensational collection *Verteidigung der Wölfe* (In defense of the wolves) of 1957, meteorically ascended to the rank of one of the leading postwar German poets, published a *Museum der modernen Poesie* (Museum of modern poetry) just four years after Friedrich's book; and this monumental and sovereign anthology, which comprises a thorough and sizable introduction as well, far transcends and supersedes the narrow, prejudiced scope of *Die Struktur der modernen Lyrik* even though it still hails Baudelaire's *Les Fleurs du mal* (The flowers of evil, 1857) as the inception of modern poetry, albeit together with Walt Whitman's *Leaves of Grass* of 1855—as does, by the way, Harald Hartung in his "Afterword" to his secular volume *Jahrhundertgedächtnis: Deutsche Lyrik im 20. Jahrhundert* (A hundred years of memories: German 20th-century poetry), which came out as late as 1998. In any case, Enzensberger's 1960 *Museum,* a representative documentation of worldwide dimensions, convincingly took into account the Slavic countries and Scandinavia as well as Hungary and even Turkey, along with Anglo-American and Latin American letters; hence, not only do poets writing in French, Spanish or Italian, and so on, make an imperative appearance here, but likewise, and more than rightly so, a considerable number of lyricists from the German-speaking countries. A full thirteen of them were in fact amassed by Enzensberger, with a total of fifty poems altogether, as opposed to the scanty five by those three authors admitted by Friedrich (for a critical as well as historical assessment, see Reinhold Grimm, " 'Once upon a Time': Some Fleeting Sidelights on Contemporary Western Poetry," *Manusya: Journal of Humanities* [Bangkok, Thailand] I/1 [March 1998]: 25–46).

Hardly any summary explanations—let alone any justifications—seem necessary. The reader should be aware, though, that we have included, in some rare and isolated instances, pertinent verses written and published before 1900 since the preceding anthology in The German Library, *German Poetry from 1750 to 1900,* ed. Robert M. Browning [German Library vol. 39]) omits them. Furthermore, as will soon become obvious, no traditional *Erlebnisdichtung*—i.e., immediate lyrical outpouring—in the vein of

19th-century Romanticism has been selected by us, but solely and exclusively poetry that we deem genuinely, or to a significant extent, modern; and it should also be noted that, in respect of the various anthologies that already exist, and that emphasize, for the most part, the first half of the 20th century, we have laid special stress on the poetic output of the century's second half. Needless to say, all Nazi or Stalinist poeticizing has been excluded—in agreement, incidentally, with the editorial policy of Hartung, whose selection, while giving tradition its due, did not aim at a comprehensive documentation, either. Those products are of poor aesthetic quality in any case. Unfortunately, however, and most regrettably indeed, the works of a few excellent poets have proved to be absolutely untranslatable, and have therefore, willy-nilly, been left out. The same applies to some poems—most notably, Paul Celan's great "Todesfuge" (Fugue of death)—that could not be included due to copyright restrictions.

In conclusion, we want to underscore what must be evident from the outset: namely, that we have not tried to arrange this amazing richness of 20th-century German poetry according to schools or movements (which are manifest anyhow). The sequence of the poets represented is a strictly chronological one, their years of birth being the only criterion—and with that, we are in harmony with Browning's edition. Thus, we do hope that our anthology will succeed both in refuting Hugo Friedrich's contentions (at least, as far as German letters are concerned) and in aptly supplementing Hans Magnus Enzensberger's seminal and, in a large measure, global *Museum*.

R. G. and I. H.

German 20th Century Poetry

Arno Holz

Aus *Phantasus*

Im Thiergarten, auf einer Bank, sitz ich und rauche;
und freue mich über die schöne Vormittagssonne.

Vor mir, glitzernd, der Kanal:
den Himmel spiegelnd, beide Ufer leise schaukelnd.

Über die Brücke, langsam Schritt, reitet ein Leutnant.

Unter ihm,
zwischen den dunklen, schwimmenden Kastanienkronen,
pfropfenzieherartig ins Wasser gedreht,
—den Kragen siegellackrot—
sein Spiegelbild.

Ein Kuckuck
ruft.

Arno Holz

From *Phantasus*

In the Thiergarten,* on a bench, I'm sitting and smoking;
and taking delight in the forenoon's lovely sunshine.

In front of me, glistening, the canal:
mirroring the sky, softly rocking either bank.

Across the bridge, at a slow walking pace, there rides a lieutenant.

Underneath him,
between the darkish, floating crowns of the chestnut trees,
coiled up in the water, corkscrew-like,
—with a collar patch red as sealing wax—
his mirror image.

A cuckoo
calls.

Translated by Reinhold Grimm

---

* "T[h]iergarten" is a famous park in downtown Berlin; as for centering the lines on
an imaginary axis of symmetry, Holz boasted of having invented it.

Richard Dehmel

Die stille Stadt

Liegt eine Stadt im Tale,
ein blasser Tag vergeht;
es wird nicht lange dauern mehr,
bis weder Mond noch Sterne,
nur Nacht am Himmel steht.

Von allen Bergen drücken
Nebel auf die Stadt;
es dringt kein Dach, nicht Hof noch Haus,
kein Laut aus ihrem Rauch heraus,
kaum Türme noch und Brücken.

Doch als den Wandrer graute,
da ging ein Lichtlein auf im Grund;
und durch den Rauch und Nebel
begann ein leiser Lobgesang
aus Kindermund.

Richard Dehmel

The Quiet Town

A town lies in the valley,
a pallid day has passed;
it won't take long till neither moon
nor stars show in the heavens,
only dark night at last.

From all the hills and ridges
fogs drift around the town;
no roof breaks through its smoke, no sound,
no yards or houses on the ground,
barely some spires and bridges.

Yet as the wanderer shuddered,
a light flared up, however dim;
and through the smoke and fogging,
there rose, intoned by children's lips,
a gentle hymn.

Translated by Reinhold Grimm

Frank Wedekind

Der blinde Knabe

Oh, ihr Tage meiner Kindheit,
Nun dahin auf immerdar,
Da die Seele noch in Blindheit,
Noch voll Licht das Auge war:
Meine Blicke ließ ich schweifen
Jedem frei ins Angesicht;
Glauben galt mir für Begreifen,
Und Gedanken kannt ich nicht.

Ich begann jedoch zu sinnen
Und zu grübeln hin und her,
Und in meiner Seele drinnen
Schwoll ein wildempörtes Meer.
Meine Blicke senkt ich nieder,
Schaute tief in mich hinein
Und erhob sie nimmer wieder
Zu dem goldnen Sonnenschein.

Mußt ich doch die Welt verachten,
Die mir Gottes Garten schien;
Denn die Guten läßt er schmachten—
Und die Bösen preisen ihn.
Freude, Lust and Ruh vergehen—
Oh, wie wohl war einst dem Kind!
Meine *Seele* hat gesehen—
Meine *Augen* wurden blind.

Frank Wedekind

The Blind Youth

Childhood days, so free of guile,
Now forever out of sight,
When my soul was blind, yet while
Still my eyes were full of light:
Freely was my glance ascending,
I looked straight into each face,
Took belief for comprehending;
Thought I did have none, those days.

But in time, I started musing,
Found the world now ill, now well,
And within me, most confusing,
A wild sea began to swell.
Now my downcast glances drifted
Deeply into my own night,
And since then were never lifted
To behold the sunny light.

What had seemed to be God's Garden,
I now recognized as base.
For the good, there is no pardon,
While the bad ones sing his praise.
Joy and cheer and peace are fleeing—
For the child, the world was kind!
Now my soul has become seeing,
And my eyes have become blind!

Translated by Felix Pollak

Max Dauthendey

Drinnen im Strauß

Der Abendhimmel leuchtet wie ein Blumenstrauß,
Wie rosige Wicken und rosa Klee sehen die Wolken aus.
Den Strauß umschließen die grünen Bäume und Wiesen,
Und leicht schwebt über der goldenen Helle
Des Mondes Sichel wie eine silberne Libelle.
Die Menschen aber gehen versunken tief drinnen im
      Strauß,
Wie die Käfer trunken und finden nicht mehr heraus.

Stefan George

[Ohne Titel]

Komm in den totgesagten park und schau:
Der schimmer ferner lächelnder gestade
Der reinen wolken unverhofftes blau
Erhellt die weiher und die bunten pfade.

Dort nimm das tiefe gelb • das weiche grau
Von birken und von buchs • der wind ist lau •
Die späten Rosen welkten noch nicht ganz •
Erlese küsse sie und flicht den kranz •

Vergiss auch diese letzten astern nicht •
Den purpur um die ranken wilder reben •
Und auch was übrig blieb von grünem leben
Verwinde leicht im herbstlichen gesicht.

Max Dauthendey

Inside the Bouquet

Like a bunch of flowers the evening sky is glowing,
Like rosy vetchlings and pink clover the clouds are showing.
Green treetops band this bouquet and green meadowland,
And gently there swims across the bright golden sky
The sickle moon like a silvery dragon fly.
The people, though, sunk into all this, walk deep inside the
     bouquet,
Like the beetles drunk with it, and have long lost their way.

Translated by Reinhold Grimm

Stefan George

[Untitled]

Come to the park they say is dead and see
The shimmer of the farther, smiling shores,
The pure clouds whose unexpected blue
Illuminates the ponds and checkered paths.

Take deep yellow, there, and tender gray
Of boxwood and of birch; the wind is mild,
And the late roses are not faded quite,
Choose and kiss them and wind them in a wreath;

And these last asters, too, do not forget,
The purple of the tendrils of wild vine
And what may still remain of living green
Lightly round the autumn vision bind.

Translated by Kenneth Gee

[Ohne Titel]

VON WELCHEN WUNDERN LACHT DIE MORGEN-ERDE
Als wär ihr erster tag? Erstauntes singen
Von neuerwachten welten trägt der wind
Verändert sieht der alten berge form
Und wie im kindheit-garten schaukeln blüten . . .
Der Strom besprengt die ufer und es schlang
Sein zitternd silber allen staub der jahre
Die schöpfung schauert wie im stand der gnade.
Kein gänger kommt des weges dessen haupt
Nicht eine ungewusste hoheit schmücke.
Ein breites licht ist übers land ergossen . . .
Heil allen die in seinen strahlen gehn!

[Untitled]

WHAT MARVELS SMILES THE MORNING-EARTH
As if it were its first day? Astonished singing
Of newly awakened worlds wind-borne
Familiar hills have changed shape
And blossoms sway as though in childhood's garden . . .
The river waters its banks, and its excited
Silver swallowed all the dust of years
Creation trembles as in the state of grace.
No walker comes along whose head
Is not adorned with unknown majesty.
Far and wide brightness is poured over the land . . .
God-speed to all who're striding in its light!

Translated by Irmgard Hunt

Else Lasker-Schüler

Mein Volk

Der Fels wird morsch,
Dem ich entspringe
Und meine Gotteslieder singe . . .
Jäh stürz ich vom Weg
Und riesele ganz in mir
Fernab, allein über Klagegestein
Dem Meer zu.

Hab mich so abgeströmt
Von meines Blutes
Mostvergorenheit.
Und immer, immer noch der Widerhall
In mir,
Wenn schauerlich gen Ost
Das morsche Felsgebein,
Mein Volk,
Zu Gott schreit.

Else Lasker-Schüler

My People

The rock grows brittle
From which I spring,
To which my canticles I sing . . .
Down I rush from the track
And inwardly only ripple
Far off, alone over wailing stone
Toward the sea.

Have flowed so much away
From the wine ferment
Of my blood.
Yet endlessly, yet even now that echo
In me,
When eastward, awesomely,
The brittle rock of bone,
My people,
Cries out to God.

Translated by Michael Hamburger

Mein blaues Klavier

Ich habe zu Hause ein blaues Klavier
Und kenne doch keine Note.

Es steht im Dunkel der Kellertür
seitdem die Welt verrohte.

Es spielen Sternenhände vier
—Die Mondfrau sang im Boote—
Nun tanzen die Ratten im Geklirr.

Zerbrochen ist die Klaviatür . . .
Ich beweine die blaue Tote.

Ach liebe Engel öffnet mir
—Ich aß vom bitteren Brote—
Mir lebend schon die Himmelstür—
Auch wider dem Verbote.

My Blue Piano

I have a blue piano at home
but I am not able to play it.

It stands in the dark of the cellar door
since the world has become barbaric.

Four sidereal hands would play
—Good luna sang in her vessel—
But now the rats dance to the din.

The keyboard is broken, silent . . .
I'm mourning the dead blue thing.

Oh dear angels open up for me
—I ate of the bitter bread—
the gate of heaven for me alive
In spite of any commandment.

Translated by Irmgard Hunt

Hugo von Hofmannsthal

Die Beiden

Sie trug den Becher in der Hand,
—ihr Kinn und Mund glich seinem Rand—,
So leicht und sicher war ihr Gang,
Kein Tropfen aus dem Becher sprang.

So leicht und fest war seine Hand:
Er ritt auf einem jungen Pferde,
Und mit nachlässiger Gebärde
Erzwang er, daß es zitternd stand.

Jedoch, wenn er aus ihrer Hand
Den leichten Becher nehmen sollte,
So war es beiden allzuschwer:
Denn beide bebten sie so sehr,
Daß keine Hand die andre fand
Und dunkler Wein am Boden rollte.

Hugo von Hofmannsthal

The Two

She bore the goblet in her hand—
her chin and mouth firm as its band—
her stride so weightless and so still
that not a drop would ever spill.

So weightless and so firm his hand:
he rode a young horse for his pleasure
and, looking like incarnate leisure,
compelled it; trembling it must stand.

But when he should take from her hand
the goblet that she lifted up,
the two were quivering so much
that each hand missed the other's touch,
and heavy grew the weightless cup
till dark wine rolled upon the sand.

Translated by Walter Kaufmann

Terzinen I: Über Vergänglichkeit

Noch spür ich ihren Atem auf den Wangen:
Wie kann das sein, daß diese nahen Tage
Fort sind, für immer fort, und ganz vergangen?

Dies ist ein Ding, das keiner voll aussinnt,
Und viel zu grauenvoll, als daß man klage:
Daß alles gleitet und vorüberrinnt.

Und daß mein eignes Ich, durch nichts gehemmt,
Herüberglitt aus einem kleinen Kind
Mir wie ein Hund unheimlich stumm und fremd.

Dann: daß ich auch vor hundert Jahren war
Und meine Ahnen, die im Totenhemd,
Mit mir verwandt sind wie mein eignes Haar,

So eins mit mir als wie mein eignes Haar.

August Stramm

Patrouille

Die Steine feinden
Fenster grinst Verrat
Äste würgen
Berge Sträucher blättern raschlig
Gellen
Tod.

Evanescence

And still upon my cheek I feel their breath.
How can it be, these days that were so near
Are gone, forever gone, to utter death?

This is a thing none thinks out to its last,
And far too terrible for any tear:
That all glides by, that all goes trickling past,

And that my self, unchecked, without pursuit,
Slipped from a little child, so sudden fast,
To grow strange as some dog to me and mute;

That I a hundred years ago was there,
And that my forbears, under grass and root,
Are mine, as close to me as my own hair,

As fully one with me as my own hair.

Translated by Herman Salinger

August Stramm

Reconnaissance Patrol

The stones inimic
Window grins betray
Branches choking
Screeny bushes leafing rustly
Yelling
Death.

Translated by Reinhold Grimm

Sturmangriff

Aus allen Winkeln gellen Fürchte Wollen
Kreisch
Peitscht
Das Leben
Vor
Sich
Her
Den keuchen Tod
Die Himmel fetzen.
Blinde schlächtert wildum das Entsetzen

Rainer Maria Rilke

Der Panther
(Im Jardin des Plantes, Paris)

Sein Blick ist vom Vorübergehn der Stäbe
so müd geworden, daß er nichts mehr hält.
Ihm ist, als ob es tausend Stäbe gäbe
und hinter tausend Stäben keine Welt.

Der weiche Gang geschmeidig starker Schritte
der sich im allerkleinsten Kreise dreht,
ist wie ein Tanz von Kraft um eine Mitte,
in der betäubt ein großer Wille steht.

Nur manchmal schiebt der Vorhang der Pupille
sich lautlos auf—. Dann geht ein Bild hinein,
geht durch der Glieder angespannte Stille—
und hört im Herzen auf zu sein.

Assault

From every corner fears resolves are yelling
Screechly
Life
Is whipping up
Be-
Fore
It
Gaspy death
The skies tear into.
Wildaround blind men are slaught by horror

Translated by Reinhold Grimm

Rainer Maria Rilke

The Panther
(Jardin des Plantes, Paris)

His gaze has been so worn by the procession
Of bars that it no longer makes a bond.
Around, a thousand bars seem to be flashing,
And in their flashing show no world beyond.

The lissom steps which round out and reenter
That tightest circuit of their running drill
Are like a dance of strength around a center
Wherein there stands benumbed a mighty will.

Only from time to time the pupil's shutter
Will draw apart: an image enters then,
To travel through the tautened body's utter
Stillness—and in the heart to end.

Translated by Walter Arndt

Die Erblindende

Sie saß so wie die anderen beim Tee.
Mir war zuerst, als ob sie ihre Tasse
ein wenig anders als die andern fasse.
Sie lächelte einmal. Es tat fast weh.

Und als man schließlich sich erhob und sprach
und langsam und wie es der Zufall brachte
durch viele Zimmer ging (man sprach und lachte),
da sah ich sie. Sie ging den andern nach,

verhalten, so wie eine, welche gleich
wird singen müssen und vor vielen Leuten;
auf ihren hellen Augen die sich freuten
war Licht von außen wie auf einem Teich.

Sie folgte langsam und sie brauchte lang,
als wäre etwas noch nicht überstiegen;
und doch: als ob, nach einem Übergang,
sie nicht mehr gehen würde, sondern fliegen.

Woman Going Blind

She sat like all the others drinking tea.
At first I sensed that she would take her cup
not quite the way the others took theirs up.
Once she did smile. It was like pain to me.

And when at last they all got up and, talking,
moved leisurely and as mere chance ordained
through many rooms (they laughed, were entertained)
—that's when I saw her, trailing in their walking,

contained, like one who is about to make
an entrance singing, watched by many faces.
On her bright eyes, so full of joy and graces,
lay light from outside, as upon a lake.

She followed slowly and passed slowly by,
as if there were still something, some omission;
and yet as if, after a brief transition,
she would be freed from walking, and would fly.

Translated by Felix Pollak

Kindheit

Da rinnt der Schule lange Angst und Zeit
mit Warten hin, mit lauter dumpfen Dingen.
O Einsamkeit, o schweres Zeitverbringen . . .
Und dann hinaus: die Straßen sprühn und klingen
und auf den Plätzen die Fontänen springen
und in den Gärten wird die Welt so weit—
Und durch das alles gehn im kleinen Kleid,
ganz anders als die andern gehn und gingen—:
O wunderliche Zeit, o Zeitverbringen,
o Einsamkeit.

Und in das alles fern hinauszuschauen:
Männer und Frauen; Männer, Männer, Frauen
und Kinder, welche anders sind und bunt;
und da ein Haus und dann und wann ein Hund
und Schrecken lautlos wechselnd mit Vertrauen—:
O Trauer ohne Sinn, o Traum, o Grauen,
o Tiefe ohne Grund.

Und so zu spielen: Ball und Ring und Reifen
in einem Garten, welcher sanft verblaßt,
und manchmal die Erwachsenen zu streifen,
blind und verwildert in des Haschens Hast,
aber am Abend still, mit kleinen steifen
Schritten nachhaus zu gehn, fest angefaßt—:
O immer mehr entweichendes Begreifen,
o Angst, o Last.

Und stundenlang am großen grauen Teiche
mit einem kleinen Segelschiff zu knien;
es zu vergessen, weil noch andre, gleiche
und schönere Segel durch die Ringe ziehn,
und denken müssen an das kleine bleiche
Gesicht, das sinkend aus dem Teiche schien—:
O Kindheit, o entgleitende Vergleiche.
Wohin? Wohin?

Childhood

The schoolday's stretching time of fear and stress
runs on in waiting, dullness to the end.
Oh loneliness, oh heavy time to spend . . .
Then out at last: streets sing and sparkle, bent
on joy, glistening plaza fountains rend
the air, and gardens grow worldwide with bliss.
And walking through all this in one's small dress
other than any others ever went—:
Oh wondrous time, oh time wondrously spent,
oh loneliness.

And looking out on all this from afar:
Men, women; women, men, men, more
and children, who are different, gay and sound;
and here a house and here and there a hound
and fear becoming trust, trust turning fear—:
Oh groundless grief, oh dream, oh weight to bear,
oh depth, depth without ground.

And so to play: with ball and ring and hoop
in a soft garden growing gently gray
and sometimes to brush swiftly a grown-up,
heedless and blind in the wild rush of play,
but in the evening still, with small stiff steps
to walk back home, held much too tight to stray—:
Oh comprehension's ever-widening gap,
oh fear, oh woe.

And then to kneel for hours on the shore
of the grey pond with a little sailboat; to
forget it over others, even more
sublime, that would glide through those ripples; to
keep thinking of the little face, which far
and pale sinks from that deep and once was you—:
Oh childhood, sinking, sinking past compare.
Whereto? Whereto?

Translated by Felix Pollak

Franz Kafka

In der abendlichen Sonne

In der abendlichen Sonne
sitzen wir gebeugten Rückens
auf den Bänken in dem Grünen.
Unsere Arme hängen nieder,
unsere Augen blinzeln traurig.

Und die Menschen gehn in Kleidern
schwankend auf dem Kies spazieren
unter diesem großen Himmel,
der von Hügeln in der Ferne
sich zu fernen Hügeln breitet.

Franz Kafka

In the Evening's Gentle Sunshine

In the evening's gentle sunshine,
with our backs hunched, we are sitting
on the benches in the verdure.
All our arms are feebly drooping,
all our eyes are sadly blinking.

And the people in their garments,
reeling, walk along the gravel
under this enormous skyscape
that extends from distant hillsides
to the hillsides in the distance.

Translated by Reinhold Grimm

Ernst Stadler

Fahrt über die Kölner Rheinbrücke bei Nacht

Der Schnellzug tastet sich und stößt die Dunkelheit entlang.
Kein Stern will vor. Die ganze Welt ist nur ein enger,
  nachtumschienter Minengang,
Darein zuweilen Förderstellen blauen Lichtes jähe Horizonte
  reißen: Feuerkreis
Von Kugellampen, Dächern, Schloten, dampfend, strömend . . .
  nur sekundenweis . . .
Und wieder alles schwarz. Als führen wir ins Eingeweid der
  Nacht zur Schicht.
Nun taumeln Lichter her . . . verirrt, trostlos vereinsamt . . .
  mehr . . . und sammeln sich . . . und werden dicht.
Gerippe grauer Häuserfronten liegen bloß, im Zwielicht
  bleichend, tot—etwas muß kommen . . . oh, ich fühl es
  schwer
Im Hirn. Eine Beklemmung singt im Blut. Dann dröhnt der
  Boden plötzlich wie ein Meer:
Wir fliegen, aufgehoben, königlich durch nachtentrissne Luft,
  hoch übern Strom. O Biegung der Millionen Lichter,
  stumme Wacht,
Vor deren blitzender Parade schwer die Wasser abwärts rollen.
  Endloses Spalier, zum Gruß gestellt bei Nacht!
Wie Fackeln stürmend! Freudiges! Salut von Schiffen über
  blauer See! Bestirntes Fest!
Wimmelnd, mit hellen Augen hingedrängt! Bis wo die Stadt mit
  letzten Häusern ihren Gast entläßt.
Und dann die langen Einsamkeiten. Nackte Ufer. Stille. Nacht.
  Besinnung. Einkehr. Kommunion. Und Glut und Drang
Zum Letzten, Segnenden. Zum Zeugungsfest. Zur Wollust. Zum
  Gebet! Zum Meer. Zum Untergang.

Ernst Stadler

On Crossing the Rhine Bridge at Cologne by Night

The express train gropes and thrusts its way through darkness.
    Not a star is out.
The whole world's nothing but a mine-road the night has railed
    about
In which at times conveyors of blue light tear sudden horizons:
    fiery sphere
Of arc-lamps, roofs and chimneys, steaming, streaming—for
    seconds only clear,
And all is black again. As though we drove into night's entrails
    to the seam.
Now lights reel into view . . . astray, disconsolate and lonely . . .
    more . . . and gather . . . and densely gleam.
Skeletons of gray housefronts are laid bare, grow pale in the
    twilight, dead—something must happen . . . O heavily
I feel it weigh on my brain. An oppression sings in the blood.
    Then all at once the ground resounds like the sea:
All royally upborne we fly through air from darkness wrested
    high up above the river. O curve of the million lights mute
    guard at the sight
Of whose flashing parade the waters go roaring down. Endless
    line presenting arms by night!
Surging on like torches! Joyful! Salute of ships over the blue sea!
    Star-jewelled, festive array!
Teeming, bright-eyes urged on! Till where the town with its last
    houses sees its guests away.
And then the long solitudes. Bare banks. And silence. Night.
    Reflection. Self-questioning. Communion. And ardor
    outward-flowing
To the end that blesses. To conception's rite. To pleasure's
    consummation. To prayer. To the sea. To self's undoing.

Translated by Michael Hamburger

Oskar Loerke

Aus: "Am Rande der Großen Stadt"

Geleit
Soll denn die Fremde schon beginnen,
Wo der eiserne Schwung der Maschinen
Nicht schwingt?
Und bleibt das Licht denn ewig drinnen
An seinem glühenden Draht?
Wer will der Glaskugel anbetend dienen?
Wohin das Götzenlicht nicht dringt,
Auch dort grünt Saat.

Drunten
Die Unterwelt wächst in die Ohren.
Am Radio durch Europa geht
Der Zeiger nach einem Trostgebet.
In einem Berg Vergangenheit verloren
Gregorianische Litanei.
Bei gelbem Wachsschein füllt die Stollen
Gepreßter Chorklang, Orgelrollen.
Die Lava dröhnt, bald kracht sie frei.
Und Weihnacht ist? Es war, als sei
Mariä Kind noch nicht geboren.

Berliner Winterabend
Häuser, trübe Tafeln, beschmiert mit brennender Schrift,
Die zuckend ruft und bettelnd beteuert.
Sterne sind in Wolken auf der Trift,
Der blaue Lein des Sommers ist längst eingescheuert.

Nackte Bäume wie Besen der Arbeitslosen.
Darüber streunt der freie Wind.
Ein Hauch von Süden macht das Auge blind:
Weit reicht der Dufthof der Mimosen.

Oskar Loerke

From: "At the Edge of the Great City"

Envoi
Must it be so? Should foreignness begin
Where the iron thrust of machines
Does not thrust?
And does light, then, for ever remain within
Its filament that glows?
Who wants to serve and adore the sphere of glass?
Where the idolatrous light does not pass
There, too, seed grows.

Down There
The underworld spreads in our ears.
On the radio through all of Europe runs
The pointer, after a solacing prayer.
Lost in a mountain of time past,
Gregorian litany.
By yellow waxlight the galleries fill
With compressed choral song, with organ swell.
The lava roars, soon will crack free.

Winter Evening, Berlin
Houses, dim boards, daubed with a searing script
That twitching calls out and begging affirms.
Stars are at pasture in clouds,
Summer's blue flax was garnered long ago.

Naked trees like brooms of the unemployed.
Above them tramps the free wind.
A breath from the south makes the eye go blind:
Very far the fragrance range of mimosa extends.

Translated by Michael Hamburger

Gottfried Benn

Untergrundbahn

Die weichen Schauer. Blütenfrühe. Wie
aus warmen Fellen kommt es aus den Wäldern.
Ein Rot schwärmt auf. Das große Blut steigt an.

Durch all den Frühling kommt die fremde Frau.
Der Strumpf am Spann ist da. Doch, wo er endet,
ist weit von mir. Ich schluchze auf der Schwelle:
laues Geblühe, fremde Feuchtigkeiten.

Oh, wie ihr Mund die laue Luft verpraßt!
Du Rosenhirn, Meer-Blut, du Götter-Zwielicht,
du Erdenbeet, wie strömen deine Hüften
so kühl den Gang hervor, in dem du gehst!

Dunkel: nun lebt es unter ihren Kleidern:
nur weißes Tier, gelöst und stummer Duft.

Ein armer Hirnhund, schwer mit Gott behangen.
Ich bin der Stirn so satt. Oh, ein Gerüste
von Blütenkolben löste sanft sie ab
und schwölle mit und schauerte und triefte.

So losgelöst. So müde. Ich will wandern.
Blutlos die Wege. Lieder aus den Gärten.
Schatten und Sintflut. Fernes Glück: ein Sterben
hin in des Meeres erlösend tiefes Blau.

Gottfried Benn

Subway Train

Lascivious shivers. Early bloom. As if
from warm furred skins it wafted from the woods.
A red swarms up. The great strong blood ascends.

Through all of Spring the alien woman walks.
The stocking, stretched, is there. But where it ends
is far from me. I sob upon the threshold:
sultry luxuriance, alien moistures teeming.

O how her mouth squanders the sultry air!
You brain of roses, sea-blood, goddess-twilight,
you bed of earth, how coolly from your hips
your stride flows out, the glide that is in your walking.

Dark: underneath her garments now it lives:
white animal only, loosed, and silent scent.

A wretched braindog, laden down with God.
My forehead wearies me. O that a frame
of clustered blooms would gently take its place,
to swell in unison and stream and shudder.

So lax, adrift. So tired. I long to wander.
The ways all bloodless. Songs that blow from gardens.
Shadows and Flood. Far joys: a languid dying
down into ocean's deep redeeming blue.

Translated by Michael Hamburger

Ein Wort

Ein Wort, ein Satz—: aus Chiffren steigen
erkanntes Leben, jäher Sinn,
die Sonne steht, die Sphären schweigen
und alles ballt sich zu ihm hin.

Ein Wort—ein Glanz, ein Flug, ein Feuer,
ein Flammenwurf, ein Sternenstrich—
und wieder Dunkel, ungeheuer,
im leeren Raum um Welt und Ich.

Georg Trakl

Traum des Bösen
(Erste Fassung)

Verhallend eines Gongs braungoldne Klänge—
Ein Liebender erwacht in schwarzen Zimmern
Die Wang' an Flammen, die im Fenster flimmern.
Am Strome blitzen Segel, Masten, Stränge.

Ein Mönch, ein schwangres Weib dort im Gedränge.
Guitarren klimpern, rote Kittel schimmern.
Kastanien schwül in goldnem Glanz verkümmern;
Schwarz ragt der Kirchen trauriges Gepränge.

Aus bleichen Masken schaut der Geist des Bösen.
Ein Platz verdämmert grauenvoll und düster;
Am Abend regt auf Inseln sich Geflüster.

Des Vogelfluges wirre Zeichen lesen
Aussätzige, die zur Nacht vielleicht verwesen.
Im Park erblicken zitternd sich Geschwister.

A Word

A word, a phrase—from ciphers rise
Life recognized, a sudden sense,
The sun stands still, mute are the skies,
And all compacts it, stark and dense.

A word—a gleam, a flight, a spark,
A thrust of flames, a stellar trace—
And then again—immense—the dark
Round world and I in empty space.

Translated by Richard Exner

Georg Trakl

Dream of Evil
(First Version)

A gong's brown-golden tones no longer loud—
A lover wakes in chambers growing dimmer,
His cheek near flames that in the window glimmer.
Upon the stream flash rigging, mast and shroud.

A monk, a pregnant woman in the crowd;
Guitars are strumming, scarlet dresses shimmer.
In golden gleam the chestnuts shrink and simmer;
The churches' mournful pomp looms black and proud.

The evil spirit peers from masks of white.
A square grows gloomy, hideous and stark;
Whispers arise on islands in the dark.

Lepers, who rot away perhaps at night,
Read convoluted omens of birdflight.
And siblings eye each other, trembling, in the park.

Translated by Robert Firmage

Abendland
(Vierte Fassung)

Else Lasker-Schüler in Verehrung

1.

Mond, als träte ein Totes
Aus blauer Höhle,
Und es fallen der Blüten
Viele über den Felsenpfad.
Silbern weint ein Krankes
Am Abendweiher,
Auf schwarzem Kahn
Hinüberstarben Liebende.

Oder es läuten die Schritte
Elis' durch den Hain
Den hyazinthenen
Wieder verhallend unter Eichen.
O des Knaben Gestalt
Geformt aus kristallenen Tränen,
Nächtigen Schatten.
Zackige Blitze erhellen die Schläfe
Die immerkühle,
Wenn am grünenden Hügel
Frühlingsgewitter ertönt.

The West
(Fourth Version)

In reverence to Else Lasker-Schüler

1.

Moon, as though something dead
stepped from a blue cavern,
And of the blossoms many
Fall across the rocky path.
Something sick weeps silver
At the evening pond;
On a black skiff
Lovers died across.

Or the footsteps of Elis
Ring through the grove,
The hyazinthine,
Fading again under oaktrees.
O the figure of the boy,
Formed of crystal tears,
Nocturnal shadows.
Jagged lightning flashes light his temples,
Ever cool,
When on the greening hill
Spring's thunderstorm sounds.

2.

So leise sind die grünen Wälder
Unsrer Heimat,
Die kristallne Woge
Hinsterbend an verfallner Mauer
Und wir haben im Schlaf geweint;
Wandern mit zögernden Schritten
An der dornigen Hecke hin
Singende im Abendsommer,
In heiliger Ruh
Des fern verstrahlenden Weinbergs;
Schatten nun im kühlen Schoß
Der Nacht, trauernde Adler.
So leise schließt ein mondener Strahl
Die purpurnen Male der Schwermut.

3.

Ihr großen Städte
Steinern aufgebaut
In der Ebene!
So sprachlos folgt
Der Heimatlose
Mit dunkler Stirne dem Wind,
Kahlen Bäumen am Hügel.
Ihr weithin dämmernden Ströme!
Gewaltig ängstet
Schaurige Abendröte
Im Sturmgewölk.
Ihr sterbenden Völker!
Bleiche Woge
Zerschellend am Strande der Nacht,
Fallende Sterne.

2.

So quiet are the green woods
Of our homeland,
The crystal surge
Dying along the crumbled wall,
And we have wept in sleep;
Along the thorny hedge
In the evening summer,
Singers, we wander with hesitant footsteps,
In the holy peace
Of the far-streaming vineyard;
Shadows now in the cool womb
Of the night, sorrowing eagles.
A lunar beam so softly closes
The purple stigmas of gloom.

3.

You great cities
Raised in stone
Upon the plain!
So speechlessly
With darkened brow
The homeless one follows the wind,
The naked trees on the hill.
You rivers glimmering in the distance!
An eerie red sunset
Frightens mightily
In the stormclouds.
You dying peoples!
A pale surge
Splintering on the shore of night,
Falling stars.

Translated by Robert Firmage

Der Schlaf
(Zweite Fassung)

Verflucht ihr dunklen Gifte,
Weißer Schlaf!
Dieser höchst seltsame Garten
Dämmernder Bäume
Erfüllt von Schlangen, Nachtfaltern,
Spinnen, Fledermäusen.
Fremdling! Dein verlorner Schatten
Im Abendrot,
Ein finsterer Korsar
Im salzigen Meer der Trübsal.
Aufflattern weiße Vögel am Nachtsaum
Über stürzenden Städten
Von Stahl.

Sleep
(Second Version)

Damn you dark poisons,
White sleep!
This highly peculiar garden
Of dusky trees,
Filled with serpents, nightmoths,
Spiders, bats.
Stranger! Your forlorn shadow
In the red sunset,
A sinister corsair
On the salt-seas of affliction.
White birds flap up by the seam of night
Over toppling cities
Of steel.

Translated by Robert Firmage

Grodek
(Zweite Fassung)

Am Abend tönen die herbstlichen Wälder
Von tödlichen Waffen, die goldnen Ebenen
Und blauen Seen, darüber die Sonne
Düstrer hinrollt; umfängt die Nacht
Sterbende Krieger, die wilde Klage
Ihrer zerbrochenen Münder.
Doch stille sammelt im Weidengrund
Rotes Gewölk, darin ein zürnender Gott wohnt
Das vergoßne Blut sich, mondne Kühle;
Alle Straßen münden in schwarze Verwesung.
Unter goldnem Gezweig der Nacht und Sternen
Es schwankt der Schwester Schatten durch den schweigenden
      Hain,
Zu grüßen die Geister der Helden, die blutenden Häupter;
Und leise tönen im Rohr die dunkeln Flöten des Herbstes.
O stolzere Trauer! ihr ehernen Altäre
Die heiße Flamme des Geistes nährt heute ein gewaltiger
      Schmerz,
Die ungebornen Enkel.

Grodek*
(Second Version)

At evening the autumnal forests drone
With deadly weapons, the golden plains
And the blue lakes, above which more somberly
The sun rolls down; the night
Embraces dying warriors, the wild lament
Of their shattered mouths.
But in the willow valley quietly
The outspilled blood collects, red clouds
In which an angry god dwells, lunar coolness;
All roads disgorge into black decay.
Beneath the golden boughs of night and stars
The sister's shadow flutters through the silent grove
To greet the heroes' spirits, their bleeding heads;
And softly in the reeds drone the dark flutes of autumn.
O prouder grief! you brazen altars;
Tonight a mighty anguish feeds the hot flame of spirit:
Unborn grandchildren.

Translated by Robert Firmage

---

*Grodek is a place in Galicia near Lwów (Lemberg) where a bloody battle raged in the fall of 1914; Georg Trakl died shortly thereafter—in all likelihood, by committing suicide.

Jakob van Hoddis (a.k.a. Hans Davidsohn)

Weltende

Dem Bürger fliegt vom spitzen Kopf der Hut,
In allen Lüften hallt es wie Geschrei.
Dachdecker stürzen ab und gehn entzwei,
Und an den Küsten—liest man—steigt die Flut.

Der Sturm ist da, die wilden Meere hupfen
An Land, um dicke Dämme zu zerdrücken.
Die meisten Menschen haben einen Schnupfen.
Die Eisenbahnen fallen von den Brücken.

Jakob van Hoddis

End of the World

From pointed pates hats fly into the blue,
All winds resound as though with muffled cries.
Steeplejacks fall from roofs and break in two,
And on the coasts—we read—the tides rise high.

The storm is here, the seas run wild and skip
on land, crushing thick bulwarks there.
Most people have a cold, their noses drip.
Trains tumble from the bridges everywhere.

Translated by Irmgard Hunt

Hans Arp

Kaspar ist tot

weh unser guter kaspar ist tot.

wer verbirgt nun die brennende fahne im wolkenzopf und schlägt täglich ein schwarzes schnippchen.

wer dreht nun die kaffeemühle im urfass.

wer lockt nun das idyllische reh aus der versteinerten tüte.

wer schneuzt nun die schiffe parapluies windeuter bienenväter ozonspindeln und entgrätet die pyramiden.

weh weh weh unser guter kaspar ist tot. heiliger bimbam kaspar ist tot.

die heufische klappern herzzerreissend vor leid in den glockenscheunen wenn man seinen vornamen ausspricht. darum seufze ich weiter seinen familiennamen kaspar kaspar kaspar.

warum hast du uns verlassen. in welche gestalt ist nun deine schöne grosse seele gewandert. bist du ein stern geworden oder eine kette aus wasser an einem heissen wirbelwind oder ein euter aus schwarzem licht oder ein durchsichtiger ziegel an der stöhnenden trommel des felsigen wesens.

jetzt vertrocknen unsere scheitel und sohlen und die feen liegen halbverkohlt auf dem scheiterhaufen.

jetzt donnert hinter der sonne die schwarze kegelbahn und keiner zieht mehr die kompasse und die räder der schiebkarren auf.

wer isst nun mit der phosphoreszierenden ratte am einsamen barfüssigen tisch.

wer verjagt nun den sirokkoko teufel wenn er die pferde verführen will.

wer erklärt uns nun die monogramme in den sternen.

seine büste wird die kamine aller wahrhaft edlen menschen zieren doch ist das kein trost und schnupftabak für einen totenkopf.

Hans Arp

Kaspar Is Dead

alas our good kaspar is dead.

who'll now hide the burning flag in the cloudpigtail and every day cock a black snook.

who'll now turn the coffeegrinder in the primeval tub.

who'll now lure the idyllic doe from the petrified paperbag.

who'll now blow the noses of ships parapluies windudders beefathers ozonespindles and who'll bone the pyramids.

alas alas alas our good kaspar is dead. saint dingdong kaspar is dead.

the grass-shark rattles his teeth heartrendingly in the bellbarns when his forename is spoken. therefore I shall go on sighing his familyname kaspar kaspar kaspar.

why hast thou forsaken us. into what form has thy great beautiful soul migrated. hast thou become a star or a chain of water hanging from a hot whirlwind or an udder of black light or a transparent tile on the groaning drum of the rocky essence.

now our tops and toes go dry and the fairies are lying halfcharred on the funeral pyre.

now the black skittle alley thunders behind the sun and nobody winds up the compasses and the pushcart wheels any more.

who'll now eat with the phosphorescent rat at the lonely bare-foot table.

who'll now shoo away the siroccoco devil when he tries to rav-ish the horses.

who'll now elucidate for us the monograms in the stars.

his bust will grace the mantelpieces of all truly noble men but that's no consolation and snuff for a death's head.

Translated by Christopher Middleton

Georg Heym

Umbra Vitae

Die Menschen stehen vorwärts in den Straßen
Und sehen auf die großen Himmelszeichen,
Wo die Kometen mit den Feuernasen
Um die gezackten Türme drohend schleichen.

Und alle Dächer sind voll Sternedeuter,
Die in den Himmel stecken große Röhren,
Und Zaubrer, wachsend aus den Bodenlöchern,
Im Dunkel schräg, die ein Gestirn beschwören.

Selbstmörder gehen nachts in großen Horden,
Die suchen vor sich ihr verlornes Wesen,
Gebückt in Süd und West, und Ost und Norden,
Den Staub zerfegend mit den Armen-Besen.

Sie sind wie Staub, der hält noch eine Weile.
Die Haare fallen schon auf ihren Wegen.
Sie springen, daß sie sterben, und in Eile,
Und sind mit totem Haupt im Feld gelegen,

Noch manchmal zappelnd. Und der Felder Tiere
Stehn um sie blind und stoßen mit dem Horne
In ihren Bauch. Sie strecken alle viere,
Begraben unter Salbei und dem Dorne.

Die Meere aber stocken. In den Wogen
Die Schiffe hängen modernd und verdrossen,
Zerstreut, und keine Strömung wird gezogen,
Und aller Himmel Höfe sind verschlossen.

Die Bäume wechseln nicht die Zeiten
Und bleiben ewig tot in ihrem Ende,
Und über die verfallnen Wege spreiten
Sie hölzern ihre langen Fingerhände.

Georg Heym

Umbra Vitae

The people on the streets draw up and stare,
While overhead huge portents cross the sky;
Round fanglike towers threatening comets flare,
Death-bearing, fiery-snouted where they fly.

On every roof astrologers abound,
Enormous tubes thrust heavenward; there are
Magicians springing up from underground,
Aslant in darkness, conjuring to a star.

Through night great hordes of suicides are hurled,
Men seeking on their way the selves they've lost;
Crook-backed they haunt all corners of the world,
And with their arms for brooms they sweep the dust.

They are as dust, keep but a little while;
And as they move their hair drops out. They run,
To hasten their slow dying. Then they fall,
And in the open fields lie prone,

But twitch a little still. Beasts of the field
Stand blindly round them, prod with horns
Their sprawling bodies till at last they yield,
Lie buried by the sagebrush, by the thorns.

But all the seas are stopped. Among the waves
The ships hang rotting, scattered, beyond hope.
No current through the water moves,
And all the courts of heaven are locked up.

Trees do not change, the seasons do not change.
Enclosed in dead finality each stands,
And over broken roads lets frigid range
Its palmless thousand-fingered hands.

Wer stirbt, der setzt sich auf, sich zu erheben,
Und eben hat er noch ein Wort gesprochen,
Auf einmal ist er fort. Wo ist sein Leben?
Und seine Augen sind wie Glas zerbrochen.

Schatten sind viele. Trübe und verborgen.
Und Träume, die an stummen Türen schleifen,
Und der erwacht, bedrückt vom Licht der Morgen,
Muß schweren Schlaf von grauen Lidern streifen.

Was kommt ihr, weiße Falter . . .*

Was kommt ihr, weiße Falter, so oft zu mir?
Ihr toten Seelen, was flattert ihr also oft
Auf meine Hand, von euerm Flügel
Haftet dann oft ein wenig Asche.

Die ihr bei Urnen wohnt, dort wo die Träume
        ruhn
In ewigen Schatten gebückt, in dem dämmrigen Raum
Wie in den Grüften Fledermäuse
Die nachts entschwirren mit Gelärme.

Ich höre oft im Schlaf der Vampire Gebell
Aus trüben Mondes Waben wie Gelächter,
Und sehe tief in leeren Höhlen
Der heimatlosen Schatten Lichter.

Was ist das Leben? Eine kurze Fackel
Umgrinst von Fratzen aus dem schwarzen Dunkel
Und manche kommen schon und strecken
Die magren Hände nach der Flamme.

Was ist das Leben? Kleines Schiff in Schluchten
Vergeßner Meere. Starrer Himmel Grauen.
Oder wie nachts auf kahlen Feldern
Verlornes Mondlicht wandert und verschwindet.

---

*Printed posthumously; title added by first editor.

The dying man sits up, as if to stand,
Just one more word a moment since he cries,
All at once he's gone. Can life so end?
And crushed to fragments are his glassy eyes.

The secret shadows thicken, darkness breaks;
Behind the speechless doors dreams watch and creep.
Burdened by light of dawn the man that wakes
Must rub from grayish eyelids leaden sleep.

Translated by Christopher Middleton

Why Do You Come, White Moths . . .

Why do you come, white moths, so oft to me?
Souls of the dead, why do you flutter so oft
Upon my hand; your wingbeat often
Leaves then a tiny trace of ashes.

You who are dwelling near urns, in a place where the dreams
    repose
Stooped in eternal shade, in the dim expanse
As on the vaults of tombs the bats
That nightly whir away in a tumult.

I oft hear in my sleep the vampires' yaps;
They sound as if the somber moon were laughing.
And I see deep in empty caverns
The candles of the homeless shadows.

What is all life? The brief flare-up of torchlights
Ringed by distorted frights out of black darkness
And some of them come close already
And with thin hands reach for the flames.

What is all life? Small vessel in abysses
Of seas forgotten. Dreadful rigid skies.
Or as at night across bare fields lost moonlight
Meanders till it disappears.

Weh dem, der jemals einen sterben sah,
Da unsichtbar in Herbstes kühler Stille
[Der Tod trat an des Kranken feuchtes Bette
Und einen scheiden hieß, da seine Gurgel]*

Wie einer rostigen Orgel [Frost und]† Pfeifen
Die letzte Luft mit Rasseln stieß von dannen.
Weh dem, der sterben sah. Er trägt für immer
Die weiße Blume bleiernen Entsetzens.

Wer schließt uns auf die Länder nach dem Tode,
Und wer das Tor der ungeheuren Rune.
Was sehn die Sterbenden, daß sie so schrecklich
Verkehren ihrer Augen blinde Weiße.

---

*Deleted by the author.
†Almost illegible; editor's emendation.

Woe unto him who once saw someone dying,
When in the calmness of cool autumn death
Unseen stepped up to the sick one's moist bed
And bade him pass away, while like the whistling

And rattling of a rusty organ pipe
His throat exhaled its last breath with a wheeze.
Woe to such witnesses. They bear forever
The pallid flower of a leaden horror.

Who will unlock the lands beyond our death
And who the gate of the gigantic rune.
What do the dying see that makes them roll
The blind white of their eyes so terribly.

Translated by Reinhold Grimm

Spitzköpfig kommt er . . .*

Spitzköpfig kommt er über die Dächer hoch
Und schleppt seine gelben Haare nach,
Der Zauberer, der still in die Himmelszimmer steigt
In vieler Gestirne gewundenem Blumenpfad.

Alle Tiere unten im Wald und Gestrüpp
Liegen mit Häuptern sauber gekämmt,
Singend den Mond-Choral. Aber die Kinder
Knien in den Bettchen in weißem Hemd.

Meiner Seele unendliche See
Ebbet langsam in sanfter Flut.
Ganz grün bin ich innen. Ich schwinde hinaus
Wie ein gläserner Luftballon.

---

*Title added by first editor.

With Pointed Head She Rises . . .

With pointed head she rises above the roofs
And drags her yellow hairs along,
The sorceress who calmly ascends to the rooms of the sky
On a winding path of flowers between many stars.

All the animals down in the thickets and woods
Are lying there with their heads neatly combed,
Singing the moon chorale. But the children
Kneel in their little beds in white shirts.

The immeasurable sea of my soul
Is slowly ebbing in a soft flow.
I'm all green inside. I'm vanishing out
Like a toy balloon made of glass.

Translated by Reinhold Grimm

Lichter gehen jetzt die Tage . . .*

Lichter gehen jetzt die Tage
In der sanften Abendröte
Und die Hecken sind gelichtet,
Drin der Städte Türme stecken
Und die buntbedachten Häuser.

Und der Mond ist eingeschlafen
Mit dem großen weißen Kopfe
Hinter einer großen Wolke.
Und die Straßen gehen bleicher
Durch die Häuser und die Gärten.

Die Gehängten aber schwanken
Freundlich oben auf den Bergen
In der schwarzen Silhouette,
Drum die Henker liegen schlafend,
Unterm Arm die feuchten Beile.

---

*Title added by first editor.

Clearer Now the Days Are Passing . . .

Clearer now the days are passing
In the gentle red of sunset
And the hedges have been cleared out
Where the cities' towers loom up
And the houses' colored rooftops.

And asleep the moon has fallen
With her head so white and giant
Far behind a giant cloudscape.
And the streets extend more palely
Twixt the houses and the gardens.

Those who have been hanged however
Dangle friendly on the mountains
As a silhouette of blackness;
Round them lie the hangmen sleeping,
Clasping to their dripping axes.

Translated by Reinhold Grimm

Alfred Lichtenstein

Der Morgen

. . . Und alle Straßen liegen glatt und glänzend da.
Nur selten hastet über sie ein fester Mann.
Ein fesches Mädchen haut sich heftig mit Papa.
Ein Bäcker sieht sich mal den schönen Himmel an.

Die tote Sonne hängt an Häusern, breit und dick.
Vier fette Weiber quietschen spitz vor einer Bar.
Ein Droschkenkutscher fällt und bricht sich das Genick.
Und alles ist langweilig hell, gesund und klar.

Ein Herr mit weisen Augen schwebt verrückt, voll Nacht,
Ein sicher Gott . . . in diesem Bild, das er vergaß,
Vielleicht nicht merkte—Murmelt manches. Stirbt. Und lacht.
Träumt von Gehirnschlag, Paralyse, Knochenfraß.

Alfred Lichtenstein

Morning

And all the streets lie snug there, clean and regular.
Only at times some brawny fellow hurries by.
A very smart young girl fights fiercely with Papa.
A baker, for a change, looks at the lovely sky.

The dead sun hangs on houses, broad as it is thick.
Four bulging women shrilly squeak outside a bar.
The driver of a cab falls down and breaks his neck.
And all is boringly bright, salubrious and clear.

A wise-eyed gentleman floats madly, full of night,
An ailing god . . . within this scene, which he forgot
Or failed to notice—Mutters something. Dies. And laughs.
Dreams of a cerebral stroke, paralysis, bone-rot.

Translated by Michael Hamburger

Franz Werfel

Der Mensch ist stumm

Ich habe dir den Abschiedskuß gegeben
Und klammre mich nervös an deine Hand.
Schon mahn ich dich, auf Dies und Jenes acht zu geben.
    Der Mensch ist stumm.

Will denn der Zug, der Zug nicht endlich pfeifen?
Mir ist, als dürfte ich dich nie mehr wiedersehn.
Ich rede runde Sätze, ohne zu begreifen:
    Der Mensch ist stumm.

Ich weiß, wenn ich dich nicht mehr hätte,
Das wär der Tod, der Tod, der Tod!
Und dennoch möcht ich fliehn. Gott, eine Zigarette!
    Der Mensch ist stumm.

Dahin! Jetzt auf der Straße würgt mich Weinen.
Verwundert blicke ich mich um.
Denn auch das Weinen sagt nicht, was wir meinen.
    Der Mensch ist stumm.

Franz Werfel

A Man Is Dumb

I've given you the farewell kiss
but grasp your hand uneasily.
I warn you to take care with that and this.
    A man is dumb.

Will not that train, that train at last depart?
I feel as though I'll see you nevermore.
I'm making that small talk, my head's not smart:
    A man is dumb.

If I had you no longer, that I know,
it would be quite the end of me, the end!
And yet I want to turn and run. A cigarette, my god!
    A man is dumb.

She's gone! Now on the street I choke back tears.
I look around myself in wonderment.
For even tears don't say that which we mean.
    A man is dumb.

                    Translated by Irmgard Hunt

Das Bleibende

Solang noch der Tatrawind leicht
Slovakische Blumen bestreicht,
Solang wirken Mädchen sie ein
In trauliche Buntstickerein.

Solang noch im bayrischen Wald
Die Axt im Morgengraun hallt,
Solang auch der Einsame sitzt,
Der Gott und die Heiligen schnitzt.

Solang auf ligurischer Fahrt
Das Meer seine Fischer gewahrt,
Solang wird am Strande es schaun
Die spitzenklöppelnden Fraun.

Ihr Völker der Erde, mich rührt
Das Bleibende, das ihr vollführt.
Ich selbst, ohne Volk ohne Land,
Stütz nun meine Stirn in die Hand.

The Lasting Things

As long as the Tatra breeze will
Caress Slovak flowers still,
Young girls will stitch them at ease
To make bright embroideries.

As long as the ax will resound
At dawn in Bavaria's ground,
The loner will carve and will paint
The Godhead and many a saint.

As long as Liguria's waves
Will see their fishermen's staves,
They'll also perceive within reach
The women's lace on the beach.

You peoples worldwide, I feel moved
By the lasting things you have proved.
But I, without people or land,
Now bury my head in my hand.

Translated by Reinhold Grimm

Yvan Goll

Reise ins Elend

Wie aber schmerzt die Menscheneinsamkeit,
Wenn Landschaften mit gleichem Leid wie du sich von dir
  wenden
Und in sich selbst versinken, dir so fremd!
Wenn klein ein Bahnhof dich in kalten Regen stößt,
Ein Güterwagen leer und ohne Zukunft dich anbettelt.
Da kriecht ein fahler Gaul auf dunklem Acker,
O, wenn der wüßte, daß du existierst
Und du ihn liebst, ihm würden Flügel blau zum Himmel wachsen.
Manchmal schaut Wasser auf zu dir mit großen Augen,
Und weil es nicht dein Lächeln sah,
Fällt's freudelos und schal in sich zurück.
So läßt du jedes dort allein. Es reißt dein Schicksal dich dahin.
Die alte Bucklige am Damm wird ewig nach dir blicken,
Untröstlich steht das schreiende Plakat am schiefen Giebel.
So läßt du alles dort allein in unerfüllter Liebesdemut
Selbst doch ein Einsamer, den eine Stadt erwartet,
In der du weinen wirst die lange Nacht im billigen Hotel.

Yvan Goll

Journey into Misery

Yet how the solitude of man torments
When landscapes with a sorrow like your own turn from you
And shrink into themselves, are so estranged!
A station, small, may push you out into cold rain,
A goods truck, empty and futureless, may ask for alms.
There on the dark ploughland crawls a sallow nag,
O if he only knew that you exist
And love him, he would sprout blue wings to heaven.
Sometimes with large eyes water may look up at you,
And since it did not see your smile,
Into itself it falls back flat and joyless.
So you leave each thing there alone. Fate hurries you on.
The old hunchback on the road, forever she'll watch you go,
On the slant gable the loud placard stands inconsolable.
So you leave all things there alone in loving and unanswered
        humbleness,
Solitary yourself, for whom a town is waiting
Where in your cheap hotel you'll sob the long night through.

Translated by Christopher Middleton

In uralten Seen

In uralten Seen
Hausen die traurigen Fische
Mit den Augen aus Furcht

Indessen die rosa Hügel rundum tanzen
Wie die Hügel der Bibel

Auf Schaumpferdchen schaukelt
Ein kleiner Wind—

Aus unseren uralten Augen
Lächelt es golden
Doch darunter haust eine traurige Furcht

[Sans titre]

Au cinq-millième soir de notre amour
Je suis encore aussi timide:
Je tache mes gants blancs avec les myosotis
Cueillis dans l'herbe humide,
Et maladroitement j'étouffe l'hirondelle
Que j'apportai dans la poche de mon veston.
Je ne sais pas comment sourire
Pour cacher la tristesse de mon bonheur,
Et je renverse le soleil en voulant t'embrasser.

In Age-Old Lakes

In age-old lakes
The dreary fish are dwelling
With their eyes full of fear

Whereas all around the rosy hills keep dancing
Like the hills of the Bible

On tiny horses of foam there hovers
A little wind—

From our age-old eyes a golden
Smile is emerging
Yet underneath it there dwells a dreary fear

Translated by Reinhold Grimm

[Untitled]

On the five thousandth evening of our love
I'm still as timid as before:
Tainting my white gloves with the bluish
Forget-me-nots plucked from the humid grass,
And awkwardly suffocating the swallow
I brought along in the pocket of my coat.
I do not know how to smile
So as to conceal my fortunate sadness,
And I turn the sun around when I want to embrace you.

Translated by Reinhold Grimm

[Sans titre]

Je ne voudrais être
Que le cèdre devant ta maison
Qu'une branche du cèdre
Qu'une feuille de la branche
Qu'une ombre de la feuille
Que la fraîcheur de l'ombre
Qui caresse ta tempe
Pendant une seconde

Nelly Sachs

In der blauen Ferne

In der blauen Ferne,
wo die rote Apfelbaumallee wandert
mit himmelbesteigenden Wurzelfüßen,
wird die Sehnsucht destilliert
für Alle die im Tale leben.

Die Sonne, am Wegesrand liegend
mit Zauberstäben,
gebietet Halt den Reisenden.

Die bleiben stehn
im gläsernen Albtraum,
während die Grille fein kratzt
am Unsichtbaren

und der Stein seinen Staub
tanzend in Musik verwandelt.

[Untitled]

I'd like to be nothing
But the cedar in front of your house
But a branch of this cedar
But a leaf of its branch
But a shadow of this leaf
But the freshness of its shadow
Which caresses your temple
For a second

Translated by Reinhold Grimm

Nelly Sachs

In the Blue Distance

In the blue distance
where the red avenue of apple trees roams
with root-feet that climb the sky
longing is distilled
for all those who live in the valley.

The sun, lying beside the path
with magic wands,
orders travelers to stop.

They halt
in a glassy nightmare
while the cricket lightly scratches
at invisible doors.

And dancing the stone transmutes
its dust into music.

Translated by Michael Hamburger

Der Schlafwandler

Der Schlafwandler
kreisend auf seinem Stern
an der weißen Feder des Morgens
erwacht—
der Blutfleck darauf erinnerte ihn—
läßt den Mond
erschrocken fallen—
die Schneebeere zerbricht
am schwarzen Achat der Nacht—
traumbesudelt—

Kein reines Weiß auf Erden—

The Sleepwalker

The sleepwalker
circling upon his star
is awakened by
the white feather of morning—
the bloodstain on it reminds him—
startled, he drops
the moon—
the snowberry breaks
against the black agate of night
sullied with dream—

No spotless white on this earth—

Translated by Michael Hamburger

O die Schornsteine

> Und wenn diese meine Haut zerschlagen sein wird,
> so werde ich ohne mein Fleisch Gott schauen.—Hiob

O die Schornsteine
Auf den sinnreich erdachten Wohnungen des Todes,
Als Israels Leib zog aufgelöst in Rauch
Durch die Luft—
Als Essenkehrer ihn ein Stern empfing
Der schwarz wurde
Oder war es ein Sonnenstrahl?

O die Schornsteine!
Freiheitswege für Jeremias und Hiobs Staub—
Wer erdachte euch und baute Stein auf Stein
Den Weg für Flüchtlinge aus Rauch?

O die Wohnungen des Todes,
Einladend hergerichtet
Für den Wirt des Hauses, des sonst Gast war—
O ihr Finger,
Die Eingangsschwelle legend
Wie ein Messer zwischen Leben und Tod—

O ihr Schornsteine,
O ihr Finger,
Und Israels Leib im Rauch durch die Luft!

Oh Those Smokestacks

> And when this my skin will be smashed,
> yet in my flesh I shall see God.—Job*

Oh those smokestacks
Above the abodes of death, so ingeniously devised,
When Israel's body, dissolved into smoke, was drifting
Through the air—
When, as a chimney sweep, a star received it
Turning black
Or was it a ray of the sun?

Oh those smokestacks!
Paths of freedom for Jeremiah and for the dust of Job—
Who devised you and built, placing brick upon brick,
The path for refugees of smoke?

Oh those abodes of death,
Arranged so invitingly
For the host of the house who was erstwhile the guest—
Oh you fingers,
Laying the entrance threshold
Like a knife between life and death—

Oh you smokestacks,
Oh you fingers,
And Israel's body a smoke through the air!

Translated by Reinhold Grimm

---

*The epigraph of this poem, which was composed between 1940 and 1944, stems
from Job 19:26. However, Luther's rendition runs: "Und nachdem diese meine Haut
zerschlagen ist, werde ich ohne mein Fleisch Gott sehen," and that of the *Authorized
Version,* "And *though* after my skin *worms* destroy this body, yet in my flesh I shall
see God."

Mund saugend am Tod

Mund
saugend am Tod
und sternige Strahlen
mit den Geheimnissen des Blutes
fahren aus der Ader
daran Welt zur Tränke ging
und blühte

Sterben
bezieht seinen Standpunkt aus Schweigen
und das blicklose Auge
der aussichtslosen Staubverlassenheit
tritt über die Schwelle des Sehens
während das Drama der Zeit
eingesegnet wird
dicht hinter seinem eisigen Schweißtuch.

Mouth Sucking in Death

Mouth
sucking in death,
and starry rays
replete with blood's many and manifold secrets
emanate from that vein
where the world went as for its watering place
and blossomed

Dying
obtains its standpoint from silence,
and the viewless eye
of the desperate abandonment of dust
crosses the threshold of seeing
while the drama of time
is being consecrated
right behind its icy sudary.

Translated by Reinhold Grimm

Gertrud Kolmar

Das Einhorn

Der Pfauen Pracht,
Blau, grün und gülden, blühte in Dämmerung
Tropischer Wipfelwirrnis, und graue Affen
Fletschten und zankten, hangelten, tummelten, balgten sich im
    Geschlinge.
Der große Tiger, geduckt, zuckte die Kralle, starrte, verhielt,
Als das stumme seltsame Wild durch seine indischen Wälder
    floh,
Westwärts zum Meere.

Das Einhorn.

Seine Hufe schlugen die Flut
Leicht, nur spielend. Wogen bäumten sich
Übermütig,
Und es lief mit der wiehernd springenden, jagenden
    silbermähnigen Herde.
Über ihnen
Schrieb Flug schwarzer Störche eilige Rätselzeichen an den
    Himmel Arabiens,
Der mit sinkender Sonne eine Fruchtschale bot:
Gelbe Birnen, gerötete Äpfel,
Pfirsich, Orange und prangende Trauben,
Scheiben reifer Melone.
Schwarze Felsen glommen im Untergange,
Amethystene Burgen,
Weiße glühten, verzauberte Schlösser aus Karneol und Topas.
Spät hingen Rosennebel über den taubenfarb dunkelnden
    Wassern der Bucht.

Das Einhorn.

Gertrud Kolmar

The Unicorn

The peacocks' radiance,
Blue, green and golden, blossomed in the shade
Of tangled jungle treetops, and gray monkeys
Scuffled, snarled, dangled, jumped and frolicked in the vines.
The giant tiger, crouching, curled his claws and stared and
      waited,
As that strange silent creature fled through Indian forests
Westward to the sea.

The unicorn.

His hooves pranced on the water
Softly, just playfully. The waves reared up,
High-spirited,
And on he ran beside the hurtling, racing, whinnying silver-
      maned herd.
Above them
Flights of black storks scrawled hasty enigmatic signs across
      Arabian skies,
That, with the sinking sun, became a bowl of fruit:
With yellow pears and reddish apples,
With peach and orange and resplendent grapes,
Ripe melon slices.
Black roots were glowing in the sunset
Fortresses of amethyst,
White rocks were glistening, enchanted castles of carnelian and
      topaz.
Long lay the rosy fog above the dove-gray, darkening waters of
      the bay.

The unicorn.

Seine Hufe wirbelten Sand,
Der lautlos stäubte. Es sah
Einsame Städte, bleich, mit Kuppel und Minaret und den Steinen
    der Leichenfelder
Schweigend unter dem klingenden Monde.
Es sah
Trümmer, verlassene Stätten, nur von Geistern behaust, in
    funkelnder Finsternis
Unter kalten Gestirnen.
Einmal lockte der Wüstenkauz,
Und im Fernen heulten Schakale klagend;
Hyänen lachten.
Am Eingang des Zeltes unter der Dattelpalme
Hob das weiße syrische Dromedar träumend den kleinen Kopf,
    und seine Glocke tönte.

Vorüber das Einhorn, vorüber.

Denn seine leichten, flüchtigen Füße kamen weither aus dem
    Goldlande Ophir,
Und aus seinen Augen glitzerten Blicke der Schlangen, die des
    Beschwörers Flöte aus Körben tauchen, gaukeln und tanzen
    heißt,
Doch das steile Horn seiner Stirnmitte goß sanfteres Licht,
    milchig schimmerndes,
Über die nackten Hände und weich umschleierten Brüste der Frau,
Die da stand
Zwischen Mannasträuchern.

Ihr Gruß:

Demut
Und der stille Glanz tiefer, wartender Augen
Und ein Hauchen, leise quellendes Murmeln des Mundes.—
Brunnen in Nacht.

His hooves swirled sand
That scattered soundless. And he saw
Lone cities, pale, with domes and minarets and stones of burial
    grounds,
Becalmed beneath the ringing moon.
He saw
The ruins of abandoned settlements, now only occupied by
    ghosts in sparkling darkness
Under frozen constellations.
Once the desert owl called out,
And in the distance mournful jackals howled;
Hyenas laughed.
By the entrance to the tent beneath the date palm
A silver Syrian dromedary lifted its small head from dreams and
    chimed its bell.

The unicorn ran on and on.

For his soft fleeting hooves had come from far away, out of the
    golden land of Ophir,
And from his eyes there gleamed the gaze of snakes that
    charmers' flutes dip out of baskets and command to sway
    and dance,
And yet the jutting horn upon his forehead shed a softer, milky
    shimmering light,
Across the woman's naked hands and tenderly veiled breasts
As she stood waiting
By the manna bushes.

Her greeting:
Humility
And the quiet splendor of her deep, expectant eyes,
And a breath, a gentle, welling murmur of her mouth.—
A fountain in the night.

Translated by Henry A. Smith

Bertolt Brecht

Vom armen B.B.

1.
Ich, Bertolt Brecht, bin aus den schwarzen Wäldern.
Meine Mutter trug mich in die Städte hinein
Als ich in ihrem Leibe lag. Und die Kälte der Wälder
Wird in mir bis zu meinem Absterben sein.

2.
In der Asphaltstadt bin ich daheim. Von allem Anfang
Versehen mit jedem Sterbsakrament:
Mit Zeitungen. Und Tabak. Und Branntwein.
Mißtrauisch und faul und zufrieden am End.

3.
Ich bin zu den Leuten freundlich. Ich setze
Einen steifen Hut auf nach ihrem Brauch.
Ich sage: Es sind ganz besonders riechende Tiere
Und ich sage: Es macht nichts, ich bin es auch.

4.
In meine leeren Schaukelstühle vormittags
Setze ich mir mitunter ein paar Frauen
Und ich betrachte sie sorglos und sage ihnen:
In mir habt ihr einen, auf den könnt ihr nicht bauen.

5.
Gegen Abend versammle ich um mich Männer
Wir reden uns da mit »Gentlemen« an.
Sie haben ihre Füße auf meinen Tischen
Und sagen: Es wird besser mit uns. Und ich frage nicht: Wann?

Bertolt Brecht

Of Poor B.B.

1.

I, Bertolt Brecht, came out of the black forests.
My mother moved me into the cities as I lay
Inside her body. And the coldness of the forests
Will be inside me till my dying day.

2.

In the asphalt city I'm at home. From the very start
Provided with every last sacrament:
With newspapers. And tobacco. And brandy.
To the end mistrustful, lazy and content.

3.

I'm polite and friendly to people. I put on
A hard hat because that's what they do.
I say: they are animals with a quite peculiar smell
And I say: does it matter? I am too.

4.

Before noon on my empty rocking chairs
I'll sit a woman or two, and with an untroubled eye
Look at them steadily and say to them:
Here you have someone on whom you can't rely.

5.

Towards evening it's men that I gather round me
And then we address one another as "gentlemen."
They're resting their feet on my table tops
And say: things will get better for us. And I don't ask when.

6.

Gegen Morgen in der grauen Frühe pissen die Tannen
Und ihr Ungeziefer, die Vögel, fängt an zu schrein.
Um die Stunde trink ich mein Glas in der Stadt aus und schmeiße
Den Tabakstummel weg und schlafe beunruhigt ein.

7.

Wir sind gesessen, ein leichtes Geschlechte
In Häusern, die für unzerstörbare galten
(So haben wir gebaut die langen Gehäuse des Eilands Manhattan
Und die dünnen Antennen, die das Atlantische Meer unterhalten).

8.

Von diesen Städten wird bleiben: der durch sie hindurchging, der
        Wind!
Fröhlich machet das Haus den Esser: er leert es.
Wir wissen, daß wir Vorläufige sind
Und nach uns wird kommen: nichts Nennenswertes.

9.

Bei den Erdbeben, die kommen werden, werde ich hoffentlich
Meine Virginia nicht ausgehen lassen durch Bitterkeit
Ich, Bertolt Brecht, in die Asphaltstädte verschlagen
Aus den schwarzen Wäldern in meiner Mutter in früher Zeit.

6.

In the gray light before morning the pine trees piss
And their vermin, the birds, raise their twitter and cheep.
At that hour in the city I drain my glass, then throw
The cigar butt away and worriedly go to sleep.

7.

We have sat, an easy generation
In houses held to be indestructible
(Thus we built those tall boxes on the island of Manhattan
And those thin aerials that amuse the Atlantic swell).

8.

Of those cities will remain what passed through them,
      the wind!
The house makes glad the eater: he clears it out.
We know that we're only tenants, provisional ones
And after us there will come: nothing worth talking about.

9.

In the earthquakes to come, I very much hope
I shall keep my cigar alight, embittered or no
I, Bertolt Brecht, carried off to the asphalt cities
From the black forests inside my mother long ago.

Translated by Michael Hamburger

An die Nachgeborenen

1.

Wirklich, ich lebe in finsteren Zeiten!
Das arglose Wort ist töricht. Eine glatte Stirn
Deutet auf Unempfindlichkeit hin. Der Lachende
Hat die furchtbare Nachricht
Nur noch nicht empfangen.

Was sind das für Zeiten, wo
Ein Gespräch über Bäume fast ein Verbrechen ist
Weil es ein Schweigen über so viele Untaten einschließt!
Der dort ruhig über die Straße geht
Ist wohl nicht mehr erreichbar für seine Freunde
Die in Not sind?

Es ist wahr: ich verdiene noch meinen Unterhalt
Aber glaubt mir: das ist nur ein Zufall. Nichts
Von dem, was ich tue, berechtigt mich dazu, mich sattzuessen.
Zufällig bin ich verschont. (Wenn mein Glück aussetzt, bin ich
      verloren.)

Man sagt mir: Iß und trink du! Sei froh, daß du hast!
Aber wie kann ich essen und trinken, wenn
Ich dem Hungernden entreiße, was ich esse, und
Mein Glas Wasser einem Verdurstenden fehlt?
Und doch esse und trinke ich.

Ich wäre gerne auch weise.
In den alten Büchern steht, was weise ist:
Sich aus dem Streit der Welt halten und die kurze Zeit
Ohne Furcht verbringen
Auch ohne Gewalt auskommen
Böses mit Gutem vergelten
Seine Wünsche nicht erfüllen, sondern vergessen
Gilt für weise.
Alles das kann ich nicht:
Wirklich, ich lebe in finsteren Zeiten!

To Those Born Later

1.

Truly, I live in dark times!
The guileless word is folly. A smooth forehead
Suggests insensitivity. The man who laughs
Has simply not yet had
The terrible news.

What kind of times are they, when
A talk about trees is almost a crime
Because it implies silence about so many horrors?
That man there calmly crossing the street
Is already perhaps beyond the reach of his friends
Who are in need?

It is true I still earn my keep
But, believe me, that is only an accident. Nothing
I do gives me the right to eat my fill.
By chance I've been spared. (If my luck breaks, I am
     lost.)

They say to me: Eat and drink! Be glad you have it!
But how can I eat and drink if I snatch what I eat
From the starving, and
My glass of water belongs to one dying of thirst?
And yet I eat and drink.

I would also like to be wise.
In the old books it says what wisdom is:
To shun the strife of the world and to live out
Your brief time without fear
Also to get along without violence
To return good for evil
Not to fulfil your desires but to forget them
Is accounted wise.
All this I cannot do:
Truly, I live in dark times.

2.

In die Städte kam ich zur Zeit der Unordnung
Als da Hunger herrschte.
Unter die Menschen kam ich zu der Zeit des Aufruhrs
Und ich empörte mich mit ihnen.
So verging meine Zeit
Die auf Erden mir gegeben war.

Mein Essen aß ich zwischen den Schlachten
Schlafen legte ich mich unter die Mörder
Der Liebe pflegte ich achtlos
Und die Natur sah ich ohne Geduld.
So verging meine Zeit
Die auf Erden mir gegeben war.

Die Straßen führten in den Sumpf zu meiner Zeit.
Die Sprache verriet mich dem Schlächter.
Ich vermochte nur wenig. Aber die Herrschenden
Saßen ohne mich sicherer, das hoffte ich.
So verging meine Zeit
Die auf Erden mir gegeben war.

Die Kräfte waren gering. Das Ziel
Lag in großer Ferne
Es war deutlich sichtbar, wenn auch für mich
Kaum zu erreichen.
So verging meine Zeit
Die auf Erden mir gegeben war.

3.

Ihr, die ihr auftauchen werdet aus der Flut
In der wir untergegangen sind
Gedenkt
Wenn ihr von unseren Schwächen sprecht
Auch der finsteren Zeit
Der ihr entronnen seid.

Gingen wir doch, öfter als die Schuhe die Länder wechselnd
Durch die Kriege der Klassen, verzweifelt
Wenn da nur Unrecht war und keine Empörung.

2.

I came to the cities in a time of disorder
When hunger reigned there.
I came among men in a time of revolt
And I rebelled with them.
So passed my time
Which had been given to me on earth.

My food I ate between battles
To sleep I lay down among murderers
Love I practised carelessly
And nature I looked at without patience.
So passed my time
Which had been given to me on earth.

All roads led into the mire in my time.
My tongue betrayed me to the butchers.
There was little I could do. But those in power
Sat safer without me: that was my hope.
So passed my time
Which had been given to me on earth.

Our forces were slight. Our goal
Lay far in the distance
It was clearly visible, though I myself
Was unlikely to reach it.
So passed my time
Which had been given to me on earth.

3.

You who will emerge from the flood
In which we have gone under
Remember
When you speak of our failings
The dark time too
Which you have escaped.

For we went, changing countries oftener than our shoes
Through the wars of the classes, despairing
When there was injustice only, and no rebellion.

Dabei wissen wir doch:
Auch der Haß gegen die Niedrigkeit
Verzerrt die Züge.
Auch der Zorn über das Unrecht
Macht die Stimme heiser. Ach, wir
Die wir den Boden bereiten wollten für Freundlichkeit
Konnten selber nicht freundlich sein.

Ihr aber, wenn es soweit sein wird
Daß der Mensch dem Menschen ein Helfer ist
Gedenkt unsrer
Mit Nachsicht.

Elisabeth Langgässer

Daphne

Du siehst, wo sich der Waldhang weitet,
Die Espe zitternd niederwehn,
Dem Brand des Himmels hingebreitet,
Von Gras und Habichtskraut begleitet,
Die ärmlich in den Winter gehn.

Doch auch das Dunkel einer Mauer,
Wenn sie am Saum der Städte lebt,
Berührt oft ihrer Krone Schauer,
An dem du dieser Zeiten Trauer,
Ermissest, da sie grundlos bebt.

Sie wurzelt mühsam im Gerölle,
Das sie verfolgt, indem es hält—
Und vor Begrenzung, Maß und Kelle
flieht Daphne in das Laubgefälle
Und steht am Rande unserer Welt.

And yet we know:
Hatred, even of meanness
Contorts the features.
Anger, even against injustice
Makes the voice hoarse. Oh, we
Who wanted to prepare the ground for friendliness
Could not ourselves be friendly.

But you, when the time comes at last
And man is a helper to man
Think of us
With forbearance.

Translated by John Willett et al.

Elisabeth Langgässer

Daphne

See where the wooded slope grows wide
A quaking aspen tree exfoliate
Spread out to firebrands of sky
By grass and hawk-weed joined which die
And sadly wilt into their winter late.

Even the shadows of dark walls
If growing at the edge of town
Will touch the tree top's trembling awe
You grasp the sorrow of these times of all
As causeless quakes the aspen crown.

It's barely rooted in the scree
Pursuing it just as it holds—
And from restriction, limitation, trowel flees
Daphne into the falling foliage spree
And stands there at the edge of our world.

Translated by Irmgard Hunt

Marie Luise Kaschnitz

Hiroshima

Der den Tod auf Hiroshima warf
Ging ins Kloster, läutet dort die Glocken.
Der den Tod auf Hiroshima warf
Sprang vom Stuhl in die Schlinge, erwürgte sich.
Der den Tod auf Hiroshima warf
Fiel in Wahnsinn, wehrt Gespenster ab
Hunderttausend, die ihn angehen nächtlich
Auferstandene aus Staub für ihn.

Nichts von alledem ist wahr.
Erst vor kurzem sah ich ihn
Im Garten seines Hauses vor der Stadt.
Die Hecken waren noch jung und die Rosenbüsche zierlich.
Das wächst nicht so schnell, daß sich einer verbergen könnte
Im Wald des Vergessens. Gut zu sehen war
Das nackte Vorstadthaus, die junge Frau
Die neben ihm stand im Blumenkleid
Das kleine Mädchen an ihrer Hand
Der Knabe der auf seinem Rücken saß
Und über seinem Kopf die Peitsche schwang.
Sehr gut erkennbar war er selbst
Vierbeinig auf dem Grasplatz, das Gesicht
Verzerrt von Lachen, weil der Photograph
Hinter der Hecke stand, das Auge der Welt.

Marie Luise Kaschnitz

Hiroshima

The man who dropped death on Hiroshima
Has taken vows, rings the bell in the cloister.
The man who dropped death on Hiroshima
Jumped into a noose and hanged himself.
The man who dropped death on Hiroshima
Has gone insane, fights apparitions
Made out of dust that come for him,
Hundreds of thousands every night.

None of all this is true.
Just the other day I saw him
In his front yard in the suburbs.
The hedges were still low and the rosebushes dainty.
It takes time to raise an oblivious forest
For someone to hide in. Plain to see
The new, naked house, the young wife
Beside him in her flowered dress
The little girl holding her hand
The boy who was sitting across his back
Cracking a whip over his head.
He himself was easy to recognize
On all fours on his lawn, his face
A grimace of laughter, because the photographer stood
Outside the hedge, the eye of the world.

Translated by Lisel Mueller

Nicht mutig

Die Mutigen wissen
Daß sie nicht auferstehen
Daß kein Fleisch um sie wächst
Am jüngsten Morgen
Daß sie nichts mehr erinnern
Niemandem wiederbegegnen
Daß nichts ihrer wartet
Keine Seligkeit
Keine Folter
Ich
Bin nicht mutig.

Vor der Tür

Ich verlasse
Ich stoße mich ab
Von allem
Hab meine Lust
Immer am Aufbruch
Weiß kein beßres Wort
Als dies
Lebt wohl
Lebt wie ihr wollt
Womöglich wohl
Aber jedenfalls ohne mich
Ich bin schon vor der Tür
Bin an der Luft
An die Luft gelehnt
An die tausend Stimmen
Der Einsamkeit
Atme ich tief.

Not Courageous

The courageous know
That they won't be resurrected
That no new flesh will grow around them
On doomsday morning
That they won't remember anything
Won't meet anybody again
That nothing is in store for them
No eternal bliss
No torture
I
Am not courageous.

Translated by Reinhold Grimm

Outside the Door

I'm pushing off
I leave everything
Behind
Have always delighted
In departures
Don't know a better word
Than this
Farewell
Fare as you will
Possibly well
But at any rate without me
I'm already outside the door
In the open air
Leaning against the air
Against the thousand voices
Of solitude
I draw a deep breath.

Translated by Reinhold Grimm

Ein Gedicht

Ein Gedicht, aus Worten gemacht.
Wo kommen die Worte her?
Aus den Fugen wie Asseln,
Aus dem Maistrauch wie Blüten,
Aus dem Feuer wie Pfiffe,
Was mir zufällt, nehm ich,

Es zu kämmen gegen den Strich,
Es zu paaren widernatürlich,
Es nackt zu scheren,
In Lauge zu waschen
Mein Wort

Meine Taube, mein Fremdling,
Von den Lippen zerrissen,
Vom Atem gestoßen,
In den Flugsand geschrieben

Mit seinesgleichen
Mit seinesungleichen

Zeile für Zeile,
Meine eigene Wüste
Zeile für Zeile
Mein Paradies.

A Poem

A poem made of words.
Where do the words come from?
From the cracks in the wall like wood lice,
From the shrubs of May like blossoms,
From the fire like whistling,
Whatever chances upon me, I take it,

So as to comb it against the grain,
So as to pair it perversely,
So as to shear it clear,
To soak it in lye
My word

My dove, my stranger,
Torn apart by my lips,
Pushed around by my breath,
Writ in windblown sand

Along with its likes
Along with its unlikes

Line after line,
My own desert
Line after line
My paradise.

Translated by Reinhold Grimm

Genazzano

Genazzano am Abend
Winterlich
Gläsernes Klappern
Der Eselshufe
Steilauf die Bergstadt.
Hier stand ich am Brunnen
Hier wusch ich mein Brauthemd
Hier wusch ich mein Totenhemd.
Mein Gesicht lag weiß
Im schwarzen Wasser
Im wehenden Laub der Platanen.
Meine Hände waren
Zwei Klumpen Eis
Fünf Zapfen an jeder
Die klirrten.

Rose Ausländer

Der Brunnen

Im verbrannten Hof
steht noch der Brunnen
voll Tränen

Wer weinte sie

Wer trinkt
seinen Durst leer

Genazzano

Genazzano at nightfall
Winterly
A clatter like glass
Of the donkey's hooves
Steeply up
To the town on the hilltop.
Here I stood by the fountain
Here I washed my bridal gown
Here I washed my burial gown.
My face was swimming
White in the black water
In the plane trees' wafting foliage.
My hands had become
Two lumps of ice
Five icicles each that
Were clinking.

Translated by Reinhold Grimm

Rose Ausländer

The Well

In the burnt-out courtyard
the well still stands
full of tears

Who cried them

Who will drink
its thirst to the last

Translated by Irmgard Hunt

Schlaffarben

Mit schlaffarbner Stimme
murmelt der Mond
seinen Hof

Haie rauben
im grauen Meer

Ophelia schaukelt
den Wahnsinn
von Welle zu Welle

Schlaffarbnes Mondlied
die Leier treibt
taub im Wasser

Orpheus träumt seine Leier
sucht Sang
bei den Fischen

Damit kein Licht uns liebe

Sie kamen
mit scharfen Fahnen und Pistolen
schossen alle Sterne und den Mond ab
damit kein Licht uns bliebe
damit kein Licht uns liebe

Da begruben wir die Sonne
Es war eine unendliche Sonnenfinsternis

In the Color of Sleep

In a voice the color of sleep
The moon murmurs
her aureole

Sharks maraud
in the gray sea

Ophelia cradles
her madness
from wave to wave

Moon song in the color of sleep
the lyre drifting
deaf in the water

Orpheus dreaming his lyre
seeking song
among fishes

Translated by Irmgard Hunt

So That No Light Would Remain to Love Us

They came along
with piercing banners and with pistols
shooting down all the stars and the moon as well
so that no light would remain above us
so that no light would remain to love us

It was then that we buried the sun
An infinite eclipse of the sun succeeded

Translated by Reinhold Grimm

Hans Sahl

Charterflug in die Vergangenheit

Als sie zurückkamen aus dem Exil,
drückte man ihnen eine Rose in die Hand.
Die Motoren schwiegen.
Versöhnung fand statt
auf dem Flugplatz in Tegel.
Die Nachgeborenen begrüßten die Überlebenden.
Schuldlose entschuldigten sich für
die Schuld ihrer Väter.

Als die Rose verwelkt war, flogen sie
zurück in das Exil ihrer
zweiten, dritten oder vierten Heimat.
Man sprach wieder englisch.
Getränke verwandelten sich wieder
in *drinks*.
Als sie sich der Küste von
Long Island näherten,
sahen sie die Schwäne auf der Havel
an sich vorbeiziehen,
und sie weinten.

Hans Sahl

A Charter Flight into the Past

When they returned home from exile,
a rose was pressed into everybody's hand.
The engines had stopped.
Reconciliation took place
at Berlin's Tegel Airport.
Those born later welcomed
the survivors.
The guiltless apologized for
their fathers' guilt.

When every rose had withered, they flew
back to the exile of
their second homeland, their third or fourth.
English was spoken again.
Getränke turned back into
drinks.
When their plane approached the coastline
of Long Island,
they saw the swans passing by
on the River Havel,
and they wept.

Translated by Reinhold Grimm

Peter Huchel

Chausseen

Erwürgte Abendröte
Stürzender Zeit!
Chausseen. Chausseen.
Kreuzwege der Flucht.
Wagenspuren über den Acker,
Der mit den Augen
Erschlagener Pferde
Den brennenden Himmel sah.

Nächte mit Lungen voll Rauch,
Mit hartem Atem der Fliehenden,
Wenn Schüsse
Auf die Dämmerung schlugen.
Aus zerbrochenem Tor
Trat lautlos Asche und Wind,
Ein Feuer,
Das mürrisch das Dunkel kaute.

Tote,
Über die Gleise geschleudert,
Den erstickten Schrei
Wie einen Stein am Gaumen.
Ein schwarzes
Summendes Tuch aus Fliegen
Schloß ihre Wunden.

Peter Huchel

Roads

Choked sunset glow
Of crashing time.
Roads. Roads.
Intersections of flight.
Cart tracks across the ploughed field
That with the eyes
Of killed horses
Saw the sky in flames.

Nights with lungs full of smoke,
With the hard breath of the fleeing
When shots
Struck the dusk.
Out of a broken gate
Ash and wind came without a sound,
A fire
That sullenly chewed the darkness.

Corpses,
Flung over the rail tracks,
Their stifled cry
Like a stone on the palate.
A black
Humming cloth of flies
Closed their wounds.

Translated by Michael Hamburger

[Ohne Titel]

UNTER DER BLANKEN HACKE DES MONDS
Werde ich sterben,
ohne das Alphabet der Blitze
gelernt zu haben.

Im Wasserzeichen der Nacht
die Kindheit der Mythen,
nicht zu entziffern.

Unwissend
stürz ich hinab,
zu den Knochen der Füchse geworfen.

Rom

Vollendeter Sommer,
am äußersten Rand der Sonne
beginnt schon die Finsternis.
Lorbeerverwilderungen,
dahinter aus Disteln und Steinen
ein Versteck,
das sich der Stimme
verweigert.

Transparenz
des Mittagslichtes,
Verse, die an nichts erinnern,
ein helles Wasser
berührt den Mund.

[Untitled]

UNDER THE NAKED HOE OF THE MOON
I shall perish
without having learned
the lightning bolts' alphabet.

In the watermark of night
the myths' childhood:
undecipherable.

Unwittingly
I tumble down,
Being thrown to the bones of the foxes.

Translated by Reinhold Grimm

Rome

Consummate summer,
on the utmost ring of the sun
darkness already begins.
Thickets of laurel trees,
behind them a hideout
of stones and thistles
that denies itself
to the voice.

Transparency
of the light at noon,
verses reminding you of nothing,
a limpid water
touches your mouth.

Translated by Reinhold Grimm

Aristeas II

Die Einsamkeit
der Pfähle im brackigen Wasser,
an lecker Bootswand
kratzt eine tote Ratte.
Hier sitze ich mittags,
ein alter Mann,
im Schatten des Hafenschuppens
auf einem Mühlstein.

Flußlotse einst,
doch später fuhr ich Schiffe, arme Frachten,
hoch in den Norden durch die Gezeiten.
Die Kapitäne zahlten mit Konterbande,
es ließ sich leben, Weiber genug
und Segeltuch.

Die Namen verdämmern,
keiner entziffert den Text,
der hinter meinen Augen steht.
Ich, Aristeas, Sohn des Kaystrobios,
blieb verschollen,
der Gott verbannte mich
in diesen engen schmutzigen Hafen,
wo unweit der kimmerischen Fähre
das Volk mit Fellen und Amuletten handelt.

Noch stampft die Walkmühle nachts.
Manchmal hocke ich als Krähe
dort oben in der Pappel am Fluß,
reglos in der untergehenden Sonne,
den Tod erwartend,
der auf vereisten Flößen wohnt.

Aristeas II

The loneliness
of the piles in the brackish water,
a dead rat keeps on scratching
the leaky boat's side.
Here I sit at midday,
an old man,
in the shadow of the harbor shed
on a millstone.

Once a river pilot,
yet later on I steered ships (though with scanty cargoes)
far up north through the tidal changes.
The captains were used to pay in contrabands,
it was good living, women galore
and sailcloth.

The names are fading,
no one deciphers the text
that is written behind my eyes.
I, Aristeas, son of Kaystrobios,
remained missing,
banished by a god
to this narrow dirty harbor
where close to the Cimmerian ferry
people are trading in furs and amulets.

The drumming mill still pounds at night.
Sometimes I perch as a crow
up there in the poplar tree by the river,
motionless in the rays of the setting sun,
awaiting death,
who dwells on icy rafts.

Translated by Reinhold Grimm

Günter Eich

Inventur

Dies ist meine Mütze,
dies ist mein Mantel,
hier mein Rasierzeug
im Beutel aus Leinen.

Konservenbüchse:
Mein Teller, mein Becher,
ich hab in das Weißblech
den Namen geritzt.

Geritzt hier mit diesem
kostbaren Nagel,
den vor begehrlichen
Augen ich berge.

Im Brotbeutel sind
ein Paar wollene Socken
und einiges, was ich
niemand verrate,

so dient es als Kissen
nachts meinem Kopf.
Die Pappe hier liegt
zwischen mir und der Erde.

Günter Eich

Inventory

This is my cap,
this is my coat,
here's my shaving gear
in a linen sack.

A can of rations:
my plate, my cup,
I've scratched my name
in the tin.

Scratched it with this
valuable nail
which I hide
from avid eyes.

In the foodsack is
a pair of wool socks
and something else that I
show to no one,

it all serves as a pillow
for my head at night.
The cardboard here lies
between me and the earth.

Die Bleistiftmine
lieb ich am meisten:
Tags schreibt sie mir Verse,
die nachts ich erdacht.

Dies ist mein Notizbuch,
dies meine Zeltbahn,
dies ist mein Handtuch,
dies ist mein Zwirn.

Wo ich wohne

Als ich das Fenster öffnete,
schwammen Fische ins Zimmer,
Heringe. Es schien
eben ein Schwarm vorüberzuziehen.
Auch zwischen den Birnbäumen spielten sie.
Die meisten aber
hielten sich noch im Wald,
über den Schonungen und den Kiesgruben.

Sie sind lästig. Lästiger aber sind noch
die Matrosen
(auch höhere Ränge, Steuerleute, Kapitäne),
die vielfach ans offene Fenster kommen
und um Feuer bitten für ihren schlechten Tabak.

Ich will ausziehen.

The lead in my pencil
I love most of all:
in the daytime it writes down
the verses I make at night.

This is my notebook,
this is my tarpaulin,
this is my towel,
this is my thread.

Translated by David Young

Where I Live

When I opened the window,
fish swam into the room,
herring. A whole school
seemed to be passing by.
They sported among the pear trees too.
But most of them
stayed in the forest,
above the nurseries and the gravel pits.

They are annoying. Still more annoying are
the sailors
(also higher ranks, coxswains, captains)
who frequently come to the open window
and ask for a light for their awful tobacco.

I'd like to move out.

Translated by David Young

Der Mann in der blauen Jacke

Der Mann in der blauen Jacke,
der heimgeht, die Hacke geschultert,—
ich sehe ihn hinter dem Gartenzaun.

So gingen sie abends in Kanaan,
so gehen sie heim aus den Reisfeldern von Burma,
den Kartoffeläckern von Mecklenburg,
heim aus Weinbergen Burgunds und kalifornischen Gärten.

Wenn die Lampe hinter beschlagenen Scheiben aufscheint,
neide ich ihnen ihr Glück, das ich nicht teilen muß,
den patriarchalischen Abend
mit Herdrauch, Kinderwäsche, Bescheidenheit.

Der Mann in der blauen Jacke geht heimwärts;
seine Hacke, die er geschultert hat,
gleicht in der sinkenden Dämmerung einem Gewehr.

The Man in the Blue Smock

The man in the blue smock,
going home, his hoe on his shoulder—
I see him behind the garden fence.

Thus they went at nightfall in Canaan,
thus they go home from Myanmar's rice paddies,
Mecklenburg's vast potato fields,
from the vineyards of Burgundy and the Californian orchards.

When the lamp lights up behind clouded panes,
I start envying them their bliss that I don't have to share,
their patriarchal evenings
with the smoldering hearth, with children's wash, with modesty.

The man in the blue smock on his way home:
the hoe he is carrying on his shoulder
looks, as dusk is falling, like a gun.

Translated by Reinhold Grimm

Ende eines Sommers

Wer möchte leben ohne den Trost der Bäume!

Wie gut, daß sie am Sterben teilhaben!
Die Pfirsiche sind geerntet, die Pflaumen färben sich,
während unter dem Brückenbogen die Zeit rauscht.

Dem Vogelzug vertraue ich meine Verzweiflung an.
Er mißt seinen Teil von Ewigkeit gelassen ab.
Seine Strecken
werden sichtbar im Blattwerk als dunkler Zwang,
die Bewegung der Flügel färbt die Früchte.

Es heißt Geduld haben.
Bald wird die Vogelschrift entsiegelt,
unter der Zunge ist der Pfennig zu schmecken.

The End of a Summer

Who'd want to live without the trees' consolation!

How good that they partake of dying!
The peaches have been reaped, the plums start coloring up,
while time is rushing under the arch of the bridge.

I entrust my desperation to the migrating birds.
They calmly measure off their part of eternity.
Their stretches become
visible in the foliage as a dark force,
the fruits being colored by their wings' motion.

Patience is called for.
The script of the birds will soon be unsealed,
under the tongue the obol can be tasted.

Translated by Reinhold Grimm

Ernst Meister

Es war da ein anderes Haus

Es war da
Ein anderes Haus.
Doch bevor ich eintrat,
Behangen mit aasigem Elend,
Rief ich es an:
Du wirst nicht schallen,
Haus, von obsiegendem Lachen
Über den Mann "ganz aus Wasser",
Deine Schellen nicht tönen
Über den Mann "ganz aus Lehm".

Und als ich eintrat, war
In der Tat kein Gelächter
Noch Hohn der Schellen; es war
Still.

Aber die Stille
War gefuchst auf Alarm; sie setzte
Die erzne, die sich windende dunkle
Treppe hinauf, und sofort, als
Wären sie beim Genick genommen,
Eilten die Stockwerkbewohner,
Viele Versucher ohne Augen,
Auf Pfoten die Treppe hinunter,
Mich zu umringen.

An meine Ohren hängten sie sich
Mit einem Geflüster:
Des Nichtses Wimpern,
Zeig sie, Lynkeus, uns!—

Ernst Meister

In That Place Was Another House

In that place was
Another house.
But before I entered it,
Wrapped in carious misery,
I called out to it:
You will not roar,
House, with triumphant laughter
At the man "all made of water,"
Nor sound your bells
At the man "all made of clay."

And when I entered there
Was indeed no laughter
Nor mockery of the bells; it was
Silent.

But the silence
Was set for alarm; it climbed
The iron winding dark
Stairs, and at once, as though
They had been seized by the neck,
The tenants of all the floors,
Many tempters without eyes,
Hurried downstairs on their paws
To surround me.

On my ears they hung
With a whispering:
The eyelashes of Nothingness,
Show them to us, Lynkeus—

Sagt, nachdem ich
Zeugnis abgelegt
Von diesem Wachtraum:

Ist denn wirklich,
Unbezweifelbar (und wie,
Ihr irrtet?) ich sage:
Wirklich, unbezweifelbar (und wie,
Ihr irrtet?) das Haus erbaut,
Um dessentwillen ich
Wie Gilgamesch nicht ächzen will,
Das Haus, darin mitnichten
Die Schellen hängen, das böse
Lachen lauert? Ich sage:
Wirklich, unbezweifelbar (und wie,
Ihr irrtet?)

Hab ich nicht Liebe?

Tell me, after I
Have testified
To this waking dream:

Was that house really
Indubitably (and what,
You were mistaken?) I say:
Really, indubitably (and what,
You were mistaken?) built,
For whose sake
Like Gilgamesh I would not moan,
The house in which neither
Do the bells hang, nor does the evil
Laughter lurk. I say:
Really, indubitably (and what,
You were mistaken?)

Do I not have charity?

Translated by Michael Hamburger

Hilde Domin

Rückwanderung

Gerade verlern ich
den Wert
der leeren
Konservendose.

Gerade habe ich gelernt
eine Blechdose fortzuwerfen
mit der meine Freundin Ramona
dem Gast
mit der meine Freundin Ramona
mir
das Wasser schöpft
aus dem großen irdenen Krug
in der Ecke der Hütten
wenn mich dürstet
am Rande der Welt.

Gerade lerne ich bei euch
den Wert einer leeren
Blechdose
zu vergessen.

Hilde Domin

Remigration

I am just unlearning
the value
of an empty
tin can.
I have just learned
to throw away a tin can
with which my friend Ramona
for her guest
with which my friend Ramona
for me
ladles water
from the large clay vessel
in the corner of the huts
when I thirst
at the edge of the world.
I am just learning here with you
to forget
the value of an empty
tin can.

Translated by Agnes Stein

Karl Krolow

Freier Fall

Und überhaupt: gib auf.
Aber hänge nicht gleich am Kleiderhaken
oder an der Dusche im Bad,
verschwinde noch nicht um die bekannte Ecke,
wenn es auch für dich
nichts mehr zu tun gibt.
Es ist noch etwas zu früh,
die Zunge zu zeigen
und mit steifem Glied zu baumeln.
Vorläufig scheust du noch
diesen Anblick und wartest ohne Panik
auf einen freien Fall,
der nicht endet.

Karl Krolow

Free Fall

And anyhow: give up.
But don't just yet hang down from a hook
or the shower nozzle in your bathroom,
don't kick the notorious bucket yet,
even if there's nothing for you
to do anymore.
It's still a bit early
to stick out your tongue
and dangle with a stiff member.
For the present you still shy away
from that sight and wait, without panicking,
for a free fall that
won't end.

Translated by Reinhold Grimm

Angst

Die Angst tritt auf und ab. Dein bessres Teil
ist schon verraten und verkauft.
Die Tanzmaus drehte ständig sich im Kreis,
die ich als Kind im Käfig hielt.

Sie rannte so im Kreis in ihren Tod.
Ich spüre Schwindel und ich sehe zu:
hier stirbt die eine Hand, hier stirbt ein Fuß.
Ist denn der Mensch dies kranke Tier?

Ob Hegel, Heidegger—das Sein zum Tode
oder "die öffentliche Meinung zu zersetzen":
ich fühle, wie verweslich Atmen ist,
der Tropfen Zeugung, diese dünne Spur.

Robinson

1.

Immer wieder strecke ich meine Hand
Nach einem Schiff aus.
Mit der bloßen Faust versuche ich,
Nach seinem Segel zu greifen.
Anfangs fing ich
Verschiedene Fahrzeuge, die sich
Am Horizont zeigten.
Ich fange Forellen so.
Doch der Monsun sah mir
Auf die Finger
Und ließ sie entweichen,
Oder Ruder und Kompaß
Brachen. Man muß
Mit Schiffen zart umgehen.
Darum rief ich ihnen Namen nach.
Sie lauteten immer
Wie meiner.

Fear

Fear enters, exits. And your better self
has been sold down the river anyway.
The dancing mouse used to turn round and round
that I had, as a kid, locked in a cage.

Thus it kept running to the bitter end.
I feel some dizziness and I look on:
one of my hands or feet dies here or there.
Is man, I wonder, this sick animal?

Ask Hegel, Heidegger—being as dying,
or one just "undermines public opinion":
I feel how perishable breathing is,
the droplet of begetting, this thin trace.

Translated by Reinhold Grimm

Robinson

1.

Time and again, with my hand
I reach for a ship.
With my bare fist I try
To grasp its sail.
In the beginning I caught
Various vessels appearing
On the horizon.
That's how I catch trout.
But the hurricanes kept a strict
Eye upon me and my fingers
And let them escape,
Or their rudders and compasses
Broke. One must
Handle ships gingerly.
That's why I called them names.
They always sounded
Like mine.

Jetzt lebe ich nur noch
In Gesellschaft mit dem Ungehorsam
Einiger Worte.

2.

Ich habe zu rechnen aufgehört,
Wenn ich auch noch Finger habe,
Die ich nacheinander ins salzige Wasser
Tauchen kann.

Insekten und Tabakblätter
Kennen die Zeit nicht,
Die ich früher vergeudete.
Mein letzter Nachbar,
Der das Waldhorn blies
(Er hatte es einst einem Volkslied
Listig entwendet),
Kam auf See um.

Zuweilen fällt ein bißchen Sonne
Auf den Tisch, unter den ich die Füße
Strecke.
Ich brauche keine Sehnsucht mehr
Zu haben.

3.

Diese Gewohnheit, irgendwo sehr lange
Auf einem Stuhl zu sitzen
Und zu horchen, ob es
In einem regnet
Oder in der Leber
Der Skorpion sich noch rührt!

Gezählt sind alle Blitze,
Alle Streichhölzer, die übrig blieben.

Bis man es leid ist
Und den letzten Wimpel
Im Meer versenkt.

Now I keep on living only
In the company of a couple of words'
Disobedience.

2.

I've given up counting
Even though I still have my fingers
That I can dip in the brine
One after another.

Insects and tobacco leaves
Do not know
The time I squandered back then.
My last neighbor,
Who used to play the bugle
(Cunningly, he had stolen it
Once from a folk song),
Perished at sea.

Every now and then, a bit of sunshine
Touches the table under which
I stretch out my legs.
I have no need of yearning
Any longer.

3.

That habit of sitting somewhere
On a chair for a long time
And to listen whether
It's raining inside oneself
Or the scorpion
In one's liver is still moving!

All lightning bolts have been counted,
All matches that remained.

Until one is sick of everything
And dumps the last pennant
Into the sea.

Translated by Reinhold Grimm

Der Wind im Zimmer

Unter Gelächter und Türenschlagen
Findet er ins Zimmer.
Ohne Verbeugung wirft er
Die Lampe um
Und liest in den Augen
Der feindlichen Brüder.
Im Zündholz-Licht sagt er nicht
"Guten Abend".
Er zerbricht die Köpfe
Der Vorfahren. Ihre Büsten
Kommen mit den Veilchenbucketts
In den Kehricht.
Auf einer Schulter reitet er
Die Wände entlang,
Während die Zigaretten ausgehen.
Wer ihn im Dunkeln fängt,
Wird am anderen Morgen aufwachen
Mit einer fremden Windrose im Haar.

The Wind in the Room

With roars of laughter and banging of doors
It enters the room.
Without a bow it knocks
The lamp over
And reads in the eyes
Of the hostile brothers.
In the light of matches it doesn't say
"Good evening."
It breaks the ancestors'
heads to pieces; their busts,
Together with posies of violets,
Are dumped on the dustheap.
On a shoulder it rides
Along the walls
While the cigarettes are going out.
Those catching it in the dark
will awake the next morning
with a strange wind rose in their hair.

Translated by Reinhold Grimm

Im Rückspiegel

Auf goldener Scheibe
Dreht sich uns im Rücken
Die Stadt aus Glas
Mit langschenkeligen Häusern,
Bewegungen der Autos
Vor zarten Mauern.
Die Spiegelbilder ihrer Straßenzüge
Stehen in der Luft wie Flamingos
Und kröpfen die Stille:—
Apokryphe Tiere . . .

Durch deine Augen—lebendige Teiche—
Sprengt lautlose Reiterei.
Hinter deinem Mund
Hört alles Lächeln auf,
Beginnt die Ratlosigkeit der Welt,
Beginnt die Sprachlosigkeit der Welt . . .
Dein leichtes Profil
Wird zur Wolke.
Die Flamingos werden sie lieben,
Indes ich zurückbleibe mit meinen Händen,
Die ich zum Ruf an die Lippen halte.

In the Rearview Mirror

On a golden pane
Behind us, the city
Made of glass,
With its rows of long-legged houses,
Its movements of cars, is turning
In front of delicate walls.
The mirror images of its streets
Are standing in the air like flamingos
feeding upon the silence:—
Apocryphal animals . . .

Through your eyes—living ponds—
A mute cavalry gallops.
Behind your mouth
All smiles come to an end;
The helplessness of the world begins,
The speechlessness of the world begins.
Your airy profile
Turns into a cloud.
The flamingos will love it, while I
Remain behind with my hollow hands,
Cupped around my lips for calling.

Translated by Reinhold Grimm

Johannes Bobrowski

Osten

Alle meine Träume
gehn über Ebenen, ziehn
unbetretenen Wäldern
windhell entgegen, kalten
einsamen Strömen, darüber
fernher Rufe schallen
bärtiger Schiffer—

Dort sind alle Gesänge
ohne End, im geringsten
Ding steht Gefahr, vieldeutig,—
nicht zu halten mit dem und
jenem Namen: Gefilde,
Moore, eine Schlucht; wie Verhängnis
schlägt sie hinab, bleibt, gemieden,—
dort um die niederen Hügel
fliehn die Pfade davon.

Worte gelten nicht.
Aber ein Streicheln, Grüße,
Blitz unterm dunkelnden Lid
und in der Brust jenes Ziehn;
noch als Umarmungen stärker.

Johannes Bobrowski

East

All my dreams
move across the plains, travel
windbright toward
untrodden forests, cold
lonely rivers, over which ring out
from afar the calls
of bearded boatmen—

There all songs are
without end, in the humblest
thing lies danger, ambiguous—
not to be held with this or
that name: meadows,
moors, a ravine; like doom
it strikes down, stays, avoided—
there, around the low hills
tracks run, fleeing.

Words do not count.
But a caress, greetings,
lightning flash under darkening eyelid
and in the breast that spasm;
stronger even than embraces.

Händler kommen von weit. Die
unter uns wohnen, sind Fremde.
Unsicher gehn sie, fragend,
ziellosen Straßen nach, hängen
Fähren und Brücken immer
an, als wär dort Gewisses—

Wir aber kennen uns leicht.
Unsre Gespräche steigen
alle aus gleichem Grunde.
Und im Erwarten ewig
wohnt uns das Herz.

Anruf

Hoch überm See die schweigende Nowgorod.
Noch sinne ich das wohl, und es zieht das Herz
sich mir zusammen,—und doch ist ein
Frieden bereitet in der Zerstörung.

Den aber nennen! In das zerstörte Haus
gehn nur im Traum Gedanken noch ein vom Einst—
wie Möwen überm müden Flusse,
und auch ihr Schreien zerbricht im Winde.

Noch stehen Türme, die ihrer Kuppeln Last,
zerbrochnen Kronen gleich, aus der Trümmer Leid
aufheben, doch es fügt der Himmel
nur das zertretene Bild zusammen.

Traders come from far places. Those
who live among us are strangers.
Unsure they walk, asking,
roads that lead nowhere, always
linger at ferries and bridges
as though there lay certainty—

But we with ease know each other.
Our conversations all
rise from the same ground.
And in expectation forever
our hearts live.

Translated by Michael Hamburger

Invocation

High on, above the lake, the mute Nowgorod.
I well muse on this still, and my heart contracts
in me with pain—and yet there is some
peace held ready amidst all the ruins.

But how to name it! Into the ruined house
the thoughts of Once will enter in dreams alone—
like gulls across the weary river,
even their calls being smashed by flurries.

Still, towers stay, upheaving their arches' load,
like crowns that have been smashed, from the rubble's grief;
however, only their demolished
image is joined by the sky together.

Translated by Reinhold Grimm

Verlassene Ortschaft

Über den Markt,
der leer ist, mit Hühnerflügeln
der Wind
zieht eine Spur in den Staub.

Zäune. Schräggesunken
Kreuze. Die Dohlenstimme.
Wer kommt, ein Brett auf der Schulter,
wer will das neue Sims
für die Fenster schneiden, wer
kam, einen grünen Topf
unter dem Schultertuch?

Hier geht niemand. Der Himmel
findet ein Band
liegen und hebt es auf,
die Hauswand bewächst
Moos, Nebel umfliegt
einen weißen Turm, und woher
bist du gekommen?

Über klirrende Drähte
der Weidegärten, über
die Wiese am Moorloch, Wasser
folgt dir, es füllt deine Spuren schwarz.

Deserted Village

Across the marketplace,
which is empty, the wind is drawing
a track
in the dust with chickens' wings.

Fences. Crosses, sunken
slantwise. The voice of the jackdaw.
Who comes, with a board on his shoulder,
who wants to cut the new sill
for the windows, who has come,
carrying a green pot
underneath his scarf?

No one goes here. The sky
finds a string
lying about and picks it up;
the house's wall
is being covered by moss,
fog's drifting round a white tower, and
where did you come from?

Across the pasture gardens'
jingling wires, across the
meadow by the slough: water
follows you, filling, black, your tracks.

Translated by Reinhold Grimm

Bericht

Bajla Gelblung,
entflohen in Warschau
einem Transport aus dem Ghetto,
das Mädchen
ist gegangen durch Wälder,
bewaffnet, die Partisanin
wurde ergriffen
in Brest-Litowsk,
trug einen Militärmantel (polnisch),
wurde verhört von deutschen
Offizieren, es gibt
ein Foto, die Offiziere sind junge
Leute, tadellos uniformiert,
mit tadellosen Gesichtern,
ihre Haltung
ist einwandfrei.

Trakl

Stirn.
Der braune Balken.
Dielenbretter. Die Schritte
zum Fenster.
Das Grün großer Blätter. Zeichen,
geschrieben über den Tisch.

Die splitternde Schwelle. Und
verlassen. Langsam
hinter dem Fremdling her
unter Flügeln der Dohlen
in Gras und Staub
die Straße ohne Namen.

Report

Bajla Gelblung,
escaped in Warsaw
from a convoy out of the ghetto,
that young girl
wandered through forests, armed,
a partisan, she was
apprehended
in Brest Litovsk,
wearing a military coat (Polish),
was interrogated by German
officers, there exists
a photo, the officers are young people
in impeccable uniforms,
with impeccable faces,
their bearing is
beyond reproach.

Translated by Reinhold Grimm

Trakl

Brow.
The brown beam.
Floorboards. The steps
to the window.
The green of large leaves. Signs,
written over the table.

The splintering threshold. And
deserted. Slowly
pursuing the stranger
under the jackdaws' wings
in grass and dust
the road with no name.

Translated by Michael Hamburger

Paul Celan

Psalm

Niemand knetet uns wieder aus Erde und Lehm,
niemand bespricht unsern Staub.
Niemand.

Gelobt seist du, Niemand.
Dir zulieb wollen
wir blühn.
Dir
entgegen.

Ein Nichts
waren wir, sind wir, werden
wir bleiben, blühend:
die Nichts-, die
Niemandsrose.

Mit
dem Griffel seelenhell,
dem Staubfaden himmelswüst,
der Krone rot
vom Purpurwort, das wir sangen
über, o über
dem Dorn.

Paul Celan

Psalm

No one kneads us again out of earth and clay,
no one incants our dust.
No one.

Blesséd art thou, No One.
In thy sight would
we bloom.
In thy
spite.

A Nothing
we were, are now, and ever
shall be, blooming:
the Nothing-, the
No One's-Rose.

With
our pistil soul-bright,
our stamen heaven-waste,
our corolla red
from the purpleword we sang
over, o over
the thorn.

Translated by John Felstiner

[Ohne Titel]

EINMAL,
da hörte ich ihn,
da wusch er die Welt,
ungesehn, nachtlang,
wirklich.

Eins und Unendlich,
vernichtet,
ichten.

Licht war. Rettung.

[Ohne Titel]

NAH, IM AORTENBOGEN,
im Hellblut:
das Hellwort.

Mutter Rahel
weint nicht mehr.
Rübergetragen
alles Geweinte.

Still, in den Kranzarterien,
unumschnürt:
Ziw, jenes Licht.

[Untitled]

ONCE,
I heard him,
he was washing the world,
unseen, nightlong,
really.

One and Infinite,
annihilated,
they I'ed.

Light was. Salvation.

Translated by John Felstiner

[Untitled]

NEAR, IN THE AORTIC ARCH,
in bright blood:
the brightword.

Mother Rachel
weeps no more.
Carried across now
all of the weeping.

Still, in the coronary arteries,
unbinded:
Ziv, that light.

Translated by John Felstiner

[Ohne Titel]

DU SEI WIE DU, immer.

Stant vp Jherosalem inde erheyff dich

Auch wer das Band zerschnitt zu dir hin,

inde wirt
erluchtet

knüpfte es neu, in der Gehugnis,
Schlammbrocken schluckt ich, im Turm,
Sprache, Finster-Lisene,

kumi
ori.

Erich Fried

Logos

Das Wort ist mein Schwert
und das Wort beschwert mich

Das Wort ist mein Schild
und das Wort schilt mich

Das Wort ist fest
und das Wort ist lose

Das Wort ist mein Fest
und das Wort ist mein Los

[Untitled]

YOU BE LIKE YOU, ever.

Ryse up Ierosalem and rowse thyselfe

The very one who slashed the bond onto you,

and becume
yllumyned

knotted it new, in myndignesse,
spills of mire I swallowed, inside the tower,
speech, dark-selvedge,

kumi
ori. *

Translated by John Felstiner

---

*The concluding lines, *"kumi / ori,"* are the Hebrew original of Isaiah 51: 17
("Arise, shine").

Erich Fried

Logos

The word is my sword
and the word weighs upon me

The word is my shield
and the word scolds me

The word is fast
and the word is loose

The word is my feast
and the word is my lot

Translated by Reinhold Grimm

Einbürgerung

Weiße Hände
rotes Haar
blaue Augen

Weiße Steine
rotes Blut
blaue Lippen

Weiße Knochen
roter Sand
blauer Himmel

Naturalization*

White hands
red hair
blue eyes

White rocks
red blood
blue lips

White bones
red sand
blue sky

Translated by Reinhold Grimm

---

*This poem, both genuinely concrete and political, refers to the death of a GI during the Vietnam War.

Aufforderung zum Vergessen

> "Wenn sie doch ihre alten Ansprüche
> endlich vergessen wollten!"
> (Zionistisches Argument)

Sei nicht dumm
sagt der Wind
Die Welt dreht sich weiter
Alles ändert sich
Das Gewesene muß man vergessen
Wenn du dein Feld vergessen könntest
sagt die vergiftete Ernte
und wenn du dein weißes Haus vergessen könntest
sagt der Schutt
und wenn du den großen Krug vergessen könntest
sagen die Scherben
und wenn du den Ölbaum vergessen könntest
sagt der Baumstumpf
und die Orangenbäume
sagt der verbrannte Hain
und wenn du deine zwei Schwestern vergessen könntest
sagt der Weg zu den Gräbern
und wenn du die Schreie vergessen könntest
sagen die Ohren
dann könntest du aufhören dich in Gefahr zu begeben
dann könntest du weit wegfahren wie die Dattel im Bauch
    eines Schiffes
die gepflückt wurde und die frei ist von ihrem Baum
dann könntest du frei sein wie ein Sandkorn im Wind
endlich frei von der Heimat
die du verloren hast
Die Welt dreht sich weiter
Das Gewesene muß man vergessen
Sei nicht dumm
sagt der Wind
der herweht von deinen Vertreibern

Invitation to Forget

> "If only they would finally forget
> their old demands!"
> (Zionist argument)

Don't be stupid
says the wind
The world goes on turning
Everything changes
One must forget what has been
If you could forget your field
says the poisoned crop
and if you could forget your white house
says the rubble
and if you could forget the large pitcher
say the shards
and if you could forget the olive tree
says the tree stump
and the orange trees
says the burnt grove
and if you could forget your two sisters
says the path to the graves
and if you could forget the screams
say the ears
then you could stop courting danger
then you could sail far away like a date in the bilge of a ship
that has been plucked and is free of its tree
then you could be free like a grain of sand in the wind
free at last of your native land
which you have lost
The world goes on turning
One must forget what has been
Don't be stupid
says the wind
blowing across from those who drove you away

Translated by Stuart Hood

Rückblick

Ich wollte
meiner Zeit
Flamme sein
oder
Teil ihrer Flamme

Ich war
ihr Schatten
oder
ein Teil
ihres Schattens

Meine Zeit
war die Zeit
der Wut:
Schatten der Wut

Meine Zeit
war die Zeit
der Ohnmacht:
Schatten der Ohnmacht

die Zeit
der Tyrannei:
Schatten der Tyrannei

Ich wollte
meiner Zeit
Fahne sein
oder ein
Fetzen der Fahne

Retrospect

I wanted
to be the flame
of my time
or
part of its flame

I was
its shadow
or
part
of its shadow

My time
was the time
of fury—
shadow of fury

My time
was the time
of helplessness—
shadow of helplessness

the time
of tyranny—
shadow of tyranny

I wanted
to be the banner
of my time
or a
shred of its banner

Fahne
der Flamme
der Wut
der Ohnmacht
der Tyrannei
oder ihr Fetzen
oder ein Teil
seines Schattens

Helmut Heissenbüttel

Bruchstück III

Alle Horizonte sind rund.
Auf der platten Scheibe der Ebene bin ich
Der Mittelpunkt ferner Kirchturmspitzen.

Die Stimme des Radios sagt
FREIHEIT IST EIN DING DER UNMÖGLICHKEIT.
Es folgt
Das vierte Streichquartett von Arnold Schönberg.

Fern in meine Zelle scheint die Sonne.
Im Wind
Das Klappern der Hochbahn auf den Viadukten
Ist eine Melodie.

Unausfüllbarer Hunger nach Unausdenkbarem.
Kombination von Abfahrtzeiten
Ohne Ankunft.

Banner
of flame
of fury
of helplessness
of tyranny
or its shred
or part
of its shadow

Translated by Stuart Hood

Helmut Heissenbüttel

Fragment III

All horizons are round.
On the flat disc of the plain I am
The center of distant steeple-points.

The radio's voice says:
FREEDOM IS AN IMPOSSIBLE THING.
There follows
The fourth string quartet of Arnold Schönberg.

The sun shines into my cell far off.
In the wind
The clatter of the railway on the viaducts
Is a melody.

Insatiable hunger for the inexcogitable.
Combination of times of departure
Without arrival.

Translated by Christopher Middleton

[Ohne Titel]

einfache Sätze
während ich stehe fällt der Schatten hin
Morgensonne entwirft die erste Zeichnung
Blühn ist ein tödliches Geschäft
ich habe mich einverstanden erklärt
ich lebe

Ilse Aichinger

Winterantwort

Die Welt ist aus dem Stoff,
der Betrachtung verlangt:
keine Augen mehr,
um die weißen Wiesen zu sehen,
keine Ohren, um im Geäst
das Schwirren der Vögel zu hören.
Großmutter, wo sind deine Lippen hin,
um die Gräser zu schmecken,
und wer riecht uns den Himmel zu Ende,
wessen Wangen reiben sich heute
noch wund an den Mauern im Dorf?
Ist es nicht ein finsterer Wald,
in den wir gerieten?
Nein, Großmutter, er ist nicht finster,
ich weiß es, ich wohnte lang
bei den Kindern am Rande,
und es ist auch kein Wald.

[Untitled]

simple sentences
while I am standing here the shadow extends
the morning sun designs the initial drawing
Flowering is a fatal affair
I have declared that I am agreed
I'm living

Translated by Reinhold Grimm

Ilse Aichinger

Winter Answer

The world is of the stuff
that calls for perception:
no eyes left
to see the white meadows,
no ears to hear
the whirring of birds in the boughs.
Grandmother, what's become of your lips,
to savor the grasses,
and who will smell the sky for us all the way,
whose cheeks today
still rub themselves sore on walls in the village?
Is it not a gloomy wood
into which we have all strayed?
No, grandmother, it isn't gloomy,
I know, for a long time I've lived
with the children on the edge,
and neither is it a wood.

Translated by Michael Hamburger

Briefwechsel

Wenn die Post nachts käme
und der Mond schöbe die Kränkungen
unter die Tür:
Sie erschienen wie Engel
in ihren weißen Gewändern
und stünden still im Flur.

Walter Höllerer

Verweile einen Atemzug, unstetes Tier

Es zischt der Herbst, naß, aalgleich, im Dorngestrüpp.
Da ist roter Morast der Fuhrweg und
Klebrig der Acker. Verweile nur,
Lautlos in Furchen geduckt, Wollkugel du,
Federball in Ängsten,

Tanzenden Wirbelflugs inmitten, eingekreist.
Der aber in den Büschen am Wegrain dort
Schmatzt und jubelt und peitscht
—wie's dich mitnimmt!—die Beeren
Gegen das Feldkreuz.

Correspondence

If the post came at night
and the moon pushed those insults
under the door:
They would appear like angels
in their white array
and would stand still in the hall.

Translated by Michael Hamburger

Walter Höllerer

Tarry Awhile, Restless Bird

Fall fizzles, wet, eel-like, in thorny thickets.
The dirt road red morass and
muddy the field. Tarry awhile,
ducking silently in the furrow, you woolly ball,
shuttlecock full of fear,

encircled, dancing a whirling flight.
But the one over there in the roadside bushes
Smacking, jubilating, and beating
—how it takes you away!—the berries
against the cross in the field.

Translated by Irmgard Hunt

Der lag besonders mühelos am Rand

Der lag besonders mühelos am Rand
Des Weges. Seine Wimpern hingen
Schwer und zufrieden in die Augenschatten.
Man hätte meinen können, daß er schliefe.

Aber sein Rücken war (wir trugen ihn,
Den Schweren, etwas abseits, denn er störte sehr
Kolonnen, die sich drängten), dieser Rücken
War nur ein roter Lappen, weiter nichts.

Und seine Hand (wir konnten dann den Witz
Nicht oft erzählen, beide haben wir
Ihn schnell vergessen) hatte, wie ein Schwert,
Den hartgefrorenen Pferdemist gefaßt,

Den Apfel, gelb und starr,
Als wär es Erde oder auch ein Arm
Oder ein Kreuz, ein Gott: ich weiß nicht was.
Wir trugen ihn da weg und in den Schnee.

Particularly Effortless He Lay

Particularly effortless he lay
Beside the road. His lashes hung
Into the shadows of his eyes, content and heavy.
One might as well have thought he was asleep.

But his back was (we carried him,
And he was heavy, a bit aside, for he disturbed
The columns that were pressing on) this back
Was just a rag of red and nothing more.

His hand (we couldn't tell the joke so often
Then, in those days, and afterwards we both
Forgot it fast) had seized just like a sword
A piece of horse dung that was frozen hard,

The apple, yellow, stiff,
As if it might be earth, or else an arm,
Perhaps a cross, a god: I don't know what.
We carried him away into the snow.

Translated by Irmgard Hunt

Friederike Mayröcker

Ostia wird dich empfangen

ich werde in Ostia sein
ich werde dich dort erwarten
ich werde dich dort umarmen
ich werde deine Hände halten in Ostia
ich werde dort sein
in Ostia
ist die Mündung des Tiber
des alten Flusses

ich werde in Ostia nicht sein
ich werde dich dort nicht erwarten
ich werde dich dort nicht umarmen
ich werde deine Hände nicht halten in Ostia
ich werde nicht dort sein
in Ostia
ist die Mündung des alten Flusses
des Tiber

Friederike Mayröcker

Ostia Will Receive You

I'll be in Ostia
I'll be there waiting for you
I'll be there embracing you
I shall be holding your hands in Ostia
I'll be there
in Ostia
there's the mouth of the Tiber
that age-old river

I shall not be in Ostia
I shall not be there waiting for you
I shall not be there embracing you
I shan't be holding your hands in Ostia
I shall not be there
in Ostia
there's the mouth of that age-old river
the Tiber

Translated by Reinhold Grimm

Margot Scharpenberg

Rotes Tulpenfeld

So viel Rot
macht meinen Atem stocken
macht meine eigenen
Wangen glühn

so viel Werbung
von allen Seiten
die alten Sprüche
noch immer gültig
noch immer neu

reih dich ein
lieb
und laß dich lieben

Margot Scharpenberg

Field of Red Tulips

So much red
takes my breath away
makes my own cheeks
color

so much wooing
from all sides
the old slogans
still valid
still new

join the players
love
and be loved

Translation by the Author

Eugen Gomringer

Worte

worte sind schatten
schatten werden worte

worte sind spiele
spiele werden worte

sind schatten worte
werden worte spiele

sind spiele worte
werden worte schatten

sind worte schatten
werden spiele worte

sind worte spiele
werden schatten worte

Eugen Gomringer

Words

words are shadows
shadows become words

words are games
games become words

if shadows are words
words become games

if games are words
words become shadows

if words are shadows
games become words

if words are games
shadows become words

Translated by Michael Hamburger

[Konkretes Gedicht ohne Titel]

schweigen schweigen schweigen
schweigen schweigen schweigen
schweigen   schweigen
schweigen schweigen schweigen
schweigen schweigen schweigen

Wolfgang Bächler

Revolte im Spiegel

Der Maske satt, in die er jeden Morgen schlüpft,
müde des Abziehbildes einer hohlen Sicherheit,
müde den Mann zu stellen, sich ins Zeug
zu legen, sich zu setzen in die Nesselsessel,
müde sich einzuspielen, aufzuspielen,
aufzupumpen und wieder, immer wieder anzupassen,
einzupassen, korrekt, adrett, gewandt, gefaßt,
gesetzt, gewitzt, gewiegt, gewinnend,

riß er sich die Krawatte von der Brust
und schneiderte sie um zu einer Puppenschürze
für seine Tochter, zerschnitt er seinen Hut
in parallele Bänder für seinen kleinen Sohn
und ließ die Adern und die Muskeln schwellen,
bis die Manschetten platzten
und der Kragenknopf zersprang.

Sodann versetzte er seinem Spiegelbild
Kinnhaken und genau gezielte Tiefschläge
auf den Magen, in die Milz und Leber,
trat auf die Scherben, stampfte sie
zu Staub und leckte sich zufrieden
das Blut von seinen Fäusten.

[Untitled Concrete Poem]

silence silence silence
silence silence silence
silence   silence
silence silence silence
silence silence silence

Translated by Reinhold Grimm

Wolfgang Bächler

A Revolt in the Mirror

Sick of the mask he slips into every morning,
weary of the decal of hollow security,
weary of standing his ground, of putting his shoulder
to the wheel, of getting into trouble and bubble,
weary of warming up, bridling up,
showing off and, over and over again, of adapting,
adjusting himself correctly, neatly, adroitly, collectedly,
staidly, engagingly, shrewdly, astutely,

he tore his tie from his chest
and tailored it into a doll's apron
for his daughter, cut his hat
into parallel ribbons for his little son,
made his veins swell and flexed his muscles
till his cuffs burst
and his collar button splintered.

Then he landed a flourish of left and right hooks on the chin
of his mirror image and aimed precision low blows
at its stomach, its spleen and its liver,
stepped on the broken pieces, stamping
and crushing them, and, satisfied,
licked the blood off his fists.

Translated by Reinhold Grimm

Ernst Jandl

Im Delikatessenladen

bitte geben sie mir eine maiwiesenkonserve
etwas höher gelegen aber nicht zu abschüssig
so, daß man darauf noch sitzen kann.

nun, dann vielleicht eine schneehalde, tiefgekühlt
ohne wintersportler. eine fichte schön beschneit
kann dabeisein.

auch nicht. bliebe noch—hasen sehe ich haben sie da hängen.
zwei drei werden genügen. und natürlich einen jäger.
wo hängen denn die jäger?

Ernst Jandl

At the Delicatessen Shop

please give me a potted may meadow
a slightly higher altitude but not too steep
so that one can still sit on it.

all right, then, maybe a snowy slope, deep-frozen
but no skiers, please. a fir tree beautifully snowed on
can be thrown in.

you haven't? that leaves—I see you have some hares hanging there.
two or three should be enough. and a huntsman of course.
where do you hang them? I don't see the huntsmen.

Translated by Michael Hamburger

Taschen

schau, meine vielen taschen.
in dieser hab ich ansichtskarten.

in dieser zwei uhren.
meine zeit und deine zeit.

in dieser einen würfel.
23 augen sehen mehr als zwei.

du kannst dir denken
was ich an brillen schleppe.

sommerlied

wir sind die menschen auf den wiesen
bald sind wir menschen unter den wiesen
und werden wiesen, und werden wald
das wird ein heiterer landaufenthalt

Pockets

look, all those pockets of mine.
in this one I keep picture postcards.

in this one two watches
my time and your time.

in this one a die.
23 eyes see more than two.

you can imagine
how many pairs of glasses I lug around.

> *Translated by Michael Hamburger*

A summer song

we are the people in the meadows
soon we'll be people under the meadows
and we'll turn meadows, and woods we'll turn
that will be a jolly country sojourn

> *Translated by Reinhold Grimm*

Ingeborg Bachmann

Alle Tage

Der Krieg wird nicht mehr erklärt,
sondern fortgesetzt. Das Unerhörte
ist alltäglich geworden. Der Held
bleibt den Kämpfen fern. Der Schwache
ist in die Feuerzonen gerückt.
Die Uniform des Tages ist die Geduld,
die Auszeichnung der armselige Stern
der Hoffnung über dem Herzen.

Er wird verliehen,
wenn nichts mehr geschieht,
wenn das Trommelfeuer verstummt,
wenn der Feind unsichtbar geworden ist
und der Schatten ewiger Rüstung
den Himmel bedeckt.

Er wird verliehen
für die Flucht von den Fahnen,
für die Tapferkeit vor dem Freund,
für den Verrat unwürdiger Geheimnisse
und die Nichtachtung
jeglichen Befehls.

Ingeborg Bachmann

Every Day

War is no longer declared,
but is simply continued. The unheard-of
has become everyday. The hero
dodges the battle. The weak one
has moved into the firing lines.
Patience is the uniform of the day,
the high decoration: the paltry star
of hope right above one's heart.

It is awarded
when nothing occurs anymore,
when the drumfire has fallen silent,
when the enemy has turned invisible,
and an eternal armament's shadow
darkens the sky.

It is awarded
for deserting the flag,
for courage in the face of the friend,
for the disclosure of unworthy secrets
and the nonobservance
of each and every command.

Translated by Irmgard Hunt and Reinhold Grimm

Nebelland

Im Winter ist meine Geliebte
unter den Tieren des Waldes.
Daß ich vor Morgen zurückmuß,
weiß die Füchsin und lacht.
Wie die Wolken erzittern! Und mir
auf den Schneekragen fällt
eine Lage von brüchigem Eis.

Im Winter ist meine Geliebte
ein Baum unter Bäumen und lädt
die glückverlassenen Krähen
ein in ihr schönes Geäst. Sie weiß,
daß der Wind, wenn es dämmert,
ihr starres, mit Reif besetztes
Abendkleid hebt und mich heimjagt.

Im Winter ist meine Geliebte
unter den Fischen und stumm.
Hörig den Wassern, die der Strich
ihrer Flossen von innen bewegt,
steh ich am Ufer und seh,
bis mich Schollen vertreiben,
wie sie taucht und sich wendet.

Und wieder vom Jagdruf des Vogels
getroffen, der seine Schwingen
über mir steift, stürz ich
auf offenem Feld: sie entfiedert
die Hühner und wirft mir ein weißes
Schlüsselbein zu. Ich nehm's um den Hals
und geh fort durch den bitteren Flaum.

Land of Fog

In winter my loved one
stays among beasts of the forest.
That I must leave before morning
the vixen knows, and laughs.
How the clouds quiver! And down
on my snowy collar rushes
a layer of brittle ice.

In winter my loved one
is a tree among trees, and invites
crows forsaken by luck
into its beautiful branches. It knows
that the wind at dusk lifts
its stiff, frost-embroidered
evening gown, chasing me home.

In winter my loved one
is among fishes, and mute.
Spellbound by waters moved
by the streak of its fins from within,
I stand on the bank and I watch
until ice floes rush towards me
as it dives, and turns away.

And stricken again by the hunting call
of the bird spreading its pinions
above me, I fall down
in the open field: it plucks
the fowl and throws me a white
collarbone. I put it round my neck
and depart through the bitter down.

Treulos ist meine Geliebte,
ich weiß, sie schwebt manchmal
auf hohen Schuh'n nach der Stadt,
sie küßt in den Bars mit dem Strohhalm
die Gläser tief auf den Mund,
und es kommen ihr Worte für alle.
Doch diese Sprache verstehe ich nicht.

Nebelland hab ich gesehen,
Nebelherz hab ich gegessen.

Das erstgeborene Land

In mein erstgeborenes Land, in den Süden
zog ich und fand, nackt und verarmt
und bis zum Gürtel im Meer,
Stadt und Kastell.

Vom Staub in den Schlaf getreten
lag ich im Licht,
und vom ionischen Salz belaubt
hing ein Baumskelett über mir.

Da fiel kein Traum herab.

Da blüht kein Rosmarin,
kein Vogel frischt
sein Lied in Quellen auf.

In meinem erstgeborenen Land, im Süden
sprang die Viper mich an
und das Grausen im Licht.

My loved one is faithless,
I know, it sometimes floats
to the city, high-heeled, into bars,
with a drinking straw kisses
the glasses deep in the mouth,
and now finds words for them all.
But that language I don't understand.

I've seen the land of fog.
I've eaten the heart of fog.

Translated by Irmgard Hunt

The Firstborn Land

To my firstborn land, to the south
I went and found, naked, impoverished
and up to my waist in the sea,
city and citadel.

Trodden by dust into sleep,
I lay in the light,
and in foliage of Ionian salt
a skeleton tree hung above me.

No dream came down from there.

No rosemary blooms there
no bird revives
its song in the springs.

In my firstborn land, in the south
the viper attacked me
and horror in the light.

O schließ
die Augen schließ!
Preß den Mund auf den Biß!

Und als ich mich selber trank
und mein erstgeborenes Land
die Erdbeben wiegten,
war ich zum Schauen erwacht.

Da fiel mir Leben zu.

Da ist der Stein nicht tot.
Der Docht schnellt auf,
wenn ihn ein Blick entzündet.

Oh close,
close your eyes!
Press your mouth to the bite!

And as I drank myself
and earthquakes rocked
my firstborn land
I awoke in order to see.

Then life came down upon me.

There, stone is not dead.
The wick flares up
when a glance ignites it.

Translated by Irmgard Hunt

An die Sonne

Schöner als der beachtliche Mond und sein geadeltes Licht,
Schöner als die Sterne, die berühmten Orden der Nacht,
Viel schöner als der feurige Auftritt eines Kometen
Und zu weit Schönrem berufen als jedes andre Gestirn,
Weil dein und mein Leben jeden Tag an ihr hängt, ist die Sonne.

Schöne Sonne, die aufgeht, ihr Werk nicht vergessen hat
Und beendet, am schönsten im Sommer, wenn ein Tag
An den Küsten verdampft und ohne Kraft gespiegelt die Segel
Über dein Aug ziehn, bis du müde wirst und das letzte verkürzt.

Ohne die Sonne nimmt auch die Kunst wieder den Schleier,
Du erscheinst mir nicht mehr, und die See und der Sand,
Von Schatten gepeitscht, fliehen unter mein Lid.

Schönes Licht, das uns warm hält, bewahrt und wunderbar sorgt,
Daß ich wieder sehe und daß ich dich wiederseh!

Nichts Schönres unter der Sonne als unter der Sonne zu sein . . .

Nichts Schönres als den Stab im Wasser zu sehn und den Vogel
    oben,
Der seinen Flug überlegt, und unten die Fische im Schwarm,
Gefärbt, geformt, in die Welt gekommen mit einer Sendung von
    Licht
Und den Umkreis zu sehn, das Geviert eines Felds, das
    Tausendeck meines Lands
Und das Kleid, das du angetan hast. Und dein Kleid, glockig und
    blau!

Schönes Blau, in dem die Pfauen spazieren und sich verneigen,
Blau der Fernen, der Zonen des Glücks mit den Wettern für mein
    Gefühl,

A Paean to the Sun

More beautiful than the notable moon and its ennobled light,
More beautiful than the stars, night's illustrious decorations,
Much more beautiful than a comet's fiery appearance,
And destined to things far more beautiful than any other celestial
    body,
Since your life and mine depend on it every day: is the sun.

Beautiful sun that rises, never forgetting its task and
Always finishing it, most beautifully in summertime when
A day evaporates on the shores, and the sails, being mirrored
    with ease,
Are moving across your eye until you get tired and shorten the last.

Without the sun art, too, will again take the veil,
If you no longer shine for me, both the sea and the sand,
Beaten by shade, will seek refuge under my lid.

Beautiful light that keeps us warm, that maintains us and
    wondrously sees
To it that I shall see again and again see you!

Nothing more beautiful under the sun than being under the sun . . .

Nothing more beautiful than seeing the staff in the water, than
    seeing
The bird above that ponders its flight, and the shoal of fish down
    below,
Colored, formed, come into the world with a mission of light,
And seeing the circuit, a field's quadrangle, the one thousand
    parts of my land
And the dress that you've put on. And your dress, bell-shaped
    and blue!

Beautiful blue wherein the peacocks are promenading and
    bowing,
Blue of the distances, of the zones of happiness with the storms
    for my passion,

Blauer Zufall am Horizont! Und meine begeisterten Augen
Weiten sich wieder und blinken und brennen sich wund.

Schöne Sonne, der vom Staub noch die größte Bewundrung
    gebührt,
Drum werde ich nicht wegen dem Mond und den Sternen und
    nicht,
Weil die Nacht mit Kometen prahlt und in mir einen Narren
    sucht,
Sondern deinetwegen und bald endlos und wie um nichts sonst
Klage führen über den unabwendbaren Verlust meiner Augen.

Wahrlich

Für Anna Achmatova

Wem es ein Wort nie verschlagen hat,
und ich sage es euch,
wer bloß sich zu helfen weiß
und mit den Worten—

dem ist nicht zu helfen.
Über den kurzen Weg nicht
und nicht über den langen.

Einen einzigen Satz haltbar zu machen,
auszuhalten in dem Bimbam von Worten.

Es schreibt diesen Satz keiner,
der nicht unterschreibt.

Blue coincidence on the horizon! And my exultant eyes
Widen again and are gleaming and burning sore.

Beautiful sun that of all dust deserves the greatest admiration;
Therefore I shall not because of the moon and the stars, and not
Because the night parades with comets, seeking to make a fool
    of me
But for your sake, and endlessly soon, and as over nothing else
    here,
Be lamenting over the unpreventable loss of my eyes.

Translated by Reinhold Grimm

Verily

For Anna Achmatova

Whoever has never choked on a word,
And I'm telling you this,
Whoever knows only to help himself
and just with words—

cannot be helped.
Not in the short run
and not in the long run.

To make one single sentence tenable,
to endure in the babble of words.

No one will write such a sentence
who will not sign.

Translated by Irmgard Hunt

Günter Grass

Wandlung

Plötzlich waren die Kirschen da,
obgleich ich vergessen hatte,
daß es Kirschen gibt,
und verkünden ließ: Noch nie gab es Kirschen—
waren sie da, plötzlich und teuer.

Pflaumen fielen und trafen mich.
Doch wer da denkt,
ich wandelte mich,
weil etwas fiel und mich traf,
wurde noch nie von fallenden Pflaumen getroffen.

Erst als man Nüsse in meine Schuhe schüttete
und ich laufen mußte,
weil die Kinder die Kerne wollten,
schrie ich nach Kirschen, wollt ich von Pflaumen
getroffen werden—und wandelte mich ein wenig.

Günter Grass

Transformation

Suddenly there were cherries,
although I had forgotten
that cherries exist
and had proclaimed: There never were cherries—
they were there, suddenly and expensive.

Plums fell and hit me,
but whoever thinks
that I was transformed
because something fell and hit me
has never been hit by falling plums.

Only when they poured nuts into my shoes
and I had to walk
because the children wanted the kernels
I cried out for cherries, wanted plums
to hit me—and was transformed a little.

Translated by Irmgard Hunt

Danach

Vom Fisch blieb die Gräte.
Luftige Zwischenräume,
in denen die Veteranen der Revolution
mit ihrem Anhang siedeln
und Wünsche
den Grünkohl von gestern züchten.

Tauschhändler.
Wer Bauchläden voller Lösungen bot,
singt jetzt die Leere an,
bis sie Mode wird.
Viele tragen jetzt sparsam geschnittene Mäntelchen,
denen Ärmel, Knöpfe und Taschen fehlen.
Keiner will es gewesen sein.
Was spielen wir jetzt?

Eine Eingabe machen.
Sich versetzen lassen.
In welches Jahrhundert?
Einen Zopf tragen und vor Publikum abschneiden dürfen.
Oder bei Völkerwanderungen zurückbleiben,
fußkrank und bald danach ortsansässig.

Als wir anfingen, dachten wir: erst mal anfangen.
Es war ja nicht so gemeint.
Eigentlich wollten wir das und nicht das.
Aber das kam nicht.
Das kam.
Das konnten wir nicht wissen.
Das gibt es nicht.
Das liegt hinter uns.

Afterwards

Of the fish the bone remained.
Airy interstice where
the veterans of the revolution
and their followers settle,
and wishes cultivate
yesterday's kale.

Barterers who offered
vending trays of solutions
now serenade emptiness
until it becomes fashion.
Many now wear skimpy coats,
sleeves, pockets, buttons missing.
Nobody takes the blame.
What shall we play next?

Turn in an application.
Let them transfer you.
Into which century?
To wear a braid and cut it
in front of an audience.
Or in mass migrations fall behind
footsore and soon afterwards settled.

When we began, we thought: Let's just begin.
We didn't mean it that way.
Actually we wanted this and not that.
But this didn't come about.
That came about.
We couldn't have known.
This doesn't exist.
That—is past.

Was in Blubberblasen steht.
Einwürfe vom Spielfeldrand.
Warum das und nicht das?

Danach wechselte die Mode.

Ein Lernprozeß in reiner Anschauung
hat begonnen.
Wir leben anspruchslos.

In Putz geritzt bleibt.
Solange der Kot dampft,
ist die Inschrift neu.
Später gehen Sammler umher.
Kleine und längere Schreie werden aufgelesen.
Zum Beispiel dieser: Nein niemals nie!

Danach wurden die Möbel verrückt.

Diese Idee, so steil
und immer noch unbestiegen,
lockte die Bergsteiger aus aller Welt.
Sommer für Sommer verstiegen sie sich.
Schuld trugen die Zuschauer
mit ihrem: Zu hoch. Zu steil.

Die Abstände der Kastanien.
Oder mein Finger über dem engmaschigen Maschendraht.
Hier bin ich schon paarmal gelaufen.
Da hol ich mich ein.
Was reden die immer von Glück.
Froh bin ich, wenn ein Baum fehlt.
Aber regelmäßig stehen die leeren Kastanien.

What bubbles contain.
Throw-ins from out of bounds.
Why that and not this?

Afterwards, fashion changed.

A learning process of pure
pictorial instruction has begun.
We live without making demands.

Marks scratched into plaster stay.
As long as the excrement steams
the inscription is new.
Later, collectors go around.
They collect both small and longer cries,
for instance this one: No never ever!

Afterwards, the furniture was moved.

This idea, so steep
and still unconquered,
tempted climbers from all over the world.
One summer after another they went too far.
At fault were the spectators
with their: Too high. Too steep.

The distances between chestnut trees.
Or my finger above close-meshed netting wire.
Here I have walked a few times before.
Then I catch up with myself.
Always this talk about happiness. What for?
I am glad when a tree is missing.
But the empty chestnut trees stand regularly.

Schon im Davor begann das Danach.
Es sah sich gut vorbereitet
und nährte sich umsichtig im Gedränge.
Schwierig, den Schnitt
zwischen davor und danach zu ermitteln.
Denn als man Jetzt sagte, lagen schon Anträge
auf Verlegung des Jetzt vor.
(Später soll es an einem dritten Ort
teilweise stattgefunden haben.)
Danach wurden andere Dinge und Tatsachen fotografiert.

Die Flurschäden werden danach berechnet.
Danach sind wir verlegen
und suchen Witze von früher.
Danach kommen Rechnungen ins Haus.
Unsere Schulden vergessen uns nicht.

Heiner Müller

Brecht

Wirklich, er lebte in finsteren Zeiten.
Die Zeiten sind heller geworden.
Die Zeiten sind finstrer geworden.
Wenn die Helle sagt, ich bin die Finsternis
Hat sie die Wahrheit gesagt.
Wenn die Finsternis sagt, ich bin
Die Helle, lügt sie nicht.

Afterwards already began before.
It saw itself well prepared
and prudently nourished itself in the crowd.
Difficult to ascertain the line between
Before and Afterwards.
For when we said Now, proposals
for a shifting of Now had already arrived.
(Later it was said to have happened
partially in a third place.)
Afterwards, other things and facts were recorded.

Damage to crops is calculated after the fact.
Afterwards, we are embarrassed
and search for jokes from the past.
Afterwards, bills arrive.
Our debts won't forget us.

Translated by Irmgard Hunt

Heiner Müller

Brecht

Truly, he lived in dark times.
The times have brightened.
The times have darkened.
When brightness says, I am darkness,
It has told the truth.
When darkness says, I am
Brightness, it does not lie.

Translated by Reinhold Grimm

Günter Kunert

Verlorenes Venedig

Nichts mehr Nichts
außer diesen kühlen und dunklen
Gewölbebögen
mächtige Schenkel venerischer Paläste
die oben im Licht zerfallen
unterm verbröckelnden Gewand
Tiefer die völlig versteinte
Perspektive rahmt einen Streifen
Wasser
vor Alter schmutzig und träge

Eine Gondel jetzt
zöge vorbei als haltloser Traum
vergessen bevor man sich
seiner erinnert
So wäre alles Dagewesensein
zu beschreiben falls das
irgendwann irgendwem
einfiele

Günter Kunert

Venice Lost

Nothing anymore Nothing
except for those cool and dark
arches and vaults
the huge thighs of venereal palaces
decaying above in the light
under their crumbling garment
The totally petrified perspective
beneath frames a strip
of water
dirty and slow with age

A gondola now
would be passing by as a fleeting dream
forgotten before
recollected
Thus one would have to describe
whatsoever has been
if indeed that occurred
to anyone anytime

Translated by Reinhold Grimm

Theatrum mundi

Täglich treibt Ophelia
an dir vorbei. Ein Hamlet
nach dem anderen verblutet
Der Rest ist schlimmer
als Schweigen
weil Heuchelei. Du triffst sie täglich
Bruder deine Brüder
aus der Klassik und Fausti Wehklag
enthält die alten neuen Leiden
von einem der sich verkauft hat.
Der weise Nathan
hat seine Pflicht und Schuldigkeit
getan und ist verbrannt.
Macht nichts! das Publikum
erfindet selbst sich neue Juden.
Nur du und ich
beschmutzt von Furcht und Mitleid
aller Dramen
erfahren nichts als daß
wir die Komparsen sind
jenseits der Worte
die uns keiner gab.

Theatrum Mundi

Every day Ophelia
is floating past you. One Hamlet
after another is bleeding to death.
The rest is worse than
silence because
hypocrisy. You encounter them every day,
brother, your brothers
from the classical repertoire, and Faust's lament
includes the old new sorrows
of one who has sold himself.
Wise Nathan
has done his bounden duty
and has been burnt.
Never mind! The audience
will invent itself new Jews.
Only you and I
befouled with fear and pity
of all plays
learn nothing except that
we are the walk-ons
beyond the words
that nobody granted us.

Translated by Reinhold Grimm

Der jüdische Friedhof in Weißensee

Auf granitenen Platten
abgefallene Blätter. Unter ihrer Berührung
versinkt der Stein wieder
im Erdreich: Fremdland
das nur Tote einbürgert
beherrscht von den stummen Vampiren
Eiche Eibe und Lorbeer.
Mit den Zeiten unleserlich
dein Name. Niemand
lüftet mehr aus Neugier
den Efeu
über deiner Einmaligkeit.
Denn du bist zurückgekehrt
ins Rätsel
das immer unter unsteten Eindrücken
reglos und verborgen bleibt.

The Jewish Cemetery at Berlin-Weissensee

On the tombs of granite
fallen leaves. Touched by them
the stone sinks back
into the ground: a foreign land
naturalizing only the dead,
dominated by the mute vampires
of oak, yew and laurel.
Illegible, as the times go by,
your name. No one lifts anymore
out of curiosity
the ivy
covering your uniqueness.
For you have returned
into the riddle
that forever remains
motionless and hidden
under unsteady imprints.

Translated by Reinhold Grimm

Sestri Levante / Ligurien II

Leer die Hotelhalle. Bis auf
Herrn Andersen, Gefangener des Bildschirms.
Deine aufrechten Zinnsoldaten, Hans Christian,
fallen noch immer unentwegt schlachtreif,
weil es auf Erden so märchenhaft zugeht.

Und wo ein neuer Gast die Rezeption belagert:
Gediegene Leibesfülle doch
eines Haarschnitts bedürftig:
Bon Giorno, Signore Goethe, auch wieder hier?

Und sogleich und triefend
steigt und hinkt Lord Byron
an Land, Rekordschwimmer wie ehedem
olympisch.

Darum bestellt der tüchtige Geist
des Ortes einen Fotografen:
Du sollst mir ein Bild machen
von der ruhmreichen Trinität.
Auf daß der Tourist
sich vor Ehrfurcht verzehre
und seine Mahlzeit ergeben dazu.

Sestri Levante / Liguria II*

The hotel foyer empty. Except for
Mr. Andersen, prisoner of the TV screen.
Your steadfast tin soldiers fall, Hans Christian,
still incessantly ready for killing
because things on earth keep going so fabulously.

And where a new arrival besets the reception:
Distinguished corpulence, yet
in dire need of a haircut:
Buon giorno, Signor Goethe, back here again?

And at once and dripping wet
Lord Byron emerges, limping
ashore, a record swimmer, olympic
as before.

That's why the city's efficient spirit
has asked a photographer to come:
Thou shalt make unto me an image
of this glorious trinity.
So that all tourists
will wallow in awe
and humbly swallow their meals to boot.

Translated by Reinhold Grimm

---

*Sestri Levante: a place near Genoa on Italy's Eastern Riviera in the province of
Liguria.

Walter Helmut Fritz

Fast verschämt

gesteht er, daß er alte Grußkarten sammelt, daß er sie seit Jahrzehnten hortet—wie der Eichelhäher Eicheln sucht und sie als Proviant für den Winter versteckt. Grüße aus der Ferne seien ihm immer wichtig gewesen, ein paar Worte, scheinbare Nichtigkeiten, aber wenn man daran denke, daß sie alle aus einem irdischen Gastspiel kommen . . . Er zögert, erschrickt ein wenig über den Satz . . . Gut, halb seien solche Mitteilungen fadenscheinig, halb verwunschen.

Das Fiasko

Es hält uns wach. Wir lernen, ungetröstet zu leben; gefaßt zu sein auf das Schlimmste; unter Tränen zu lachen über die Ketten, die wir uns schmieden; über das, was wir einfach verpassen; über den Weg, der sich verliert; über alles, was uns über den Kopf wächst; über das Unvereinbare, das unzertrennlich ist; über die Zeit, die uns an der Nase herumführt, uns daran hindert, irgendwo Fuß zu fassen, etwas erst schenkt, dann vernichtet. Das Fiasko läßt uns verstehen, wie mitleidlos etwas in sein Gegenteil übergeht; wie schnell aus den Fugen ist, was aus den Fugen sein kann. Förderliche Allgegenwart des Fiaskos.

Walter Helmut Fritz

Almost Bashfully

he admits he has been collecting old greeting cards, storing them up
for decades—just as a jay gathers acorns and hides them as food for
the winter. Greetings from afar, he says, have always been impor-
tant to him: a couple of words, apparent trifles; but considering that
they all derive from a flying visit to earth . . . He hesitates, is star-
tled a bit by this sentence . . . Oh well, he adds, one half of such
messages is threadbare, the other half is enchanted.

Translated by Reinhold Grimm

The Fiasco

It keeps us awake. We learn how to live without consolation; to be
prepared for the worst; to laugh through our tears at the fetters
we've forged for ourselves; at the opportunities we simply miss; at
the path that disappears; at whatever we can no longer cope with; at
the incompatibilities, which are inseparable; at time playing tricks
on us, hindering us from finding a foothold, first making a gift, then
destroying it. The fiasco leads us to understand how mercilessly
things change into their opposites; how quickly whatever can be out
of joint, is out of joint. Wholesome omnipresence of the fiasco.

Translated by Reinhold Grimm

Columbus

Neulich
bin ich Columbus begegnet,
in einer Seitenstraße Genuas,
nicht weit von seinem kleinen Haus.

Er war gerade
von seiner dritten Reise zurückgekommen.

An die Existenz
eines neuen Festlandes
habe er im Grunde
nicht geglaubt, sagte er.

Die Alten
hätten ja nichts davon gewußt.

Vielmehr habe er zeitweise
den Eindruck gehabt,
er nähere sich dem Paradies.

Beobachtungen an Strömungen
hätten ihn auf den Gedanken gebracht.

Aber Kastilien war doch schöner,
meinte er.

Wenn er tatsächlich
eine neue Küste gefunden habe,
werde er es erst später verstehen.

Wenigstens besteht die Möglichkeit,
fügte er hinzu.

Columbus

The other day
I met Columbus
in a side street of Genoa,
not far from his little house.

He had just
returned from his third voyage.

As for the existence
of a new continent,
he had in effect
never believed it, he said.

The ancients,
after all, hadn't known of it.

Rather, he had at times
been under the impression
that he was approaching Paradise.

Observations of currents
had put the idea into his head.

But Castile was yet more beautiful,
he felt.

If indeed
he discovered a new coast,
he'll grasp that only later on.

At least there is a possibility,
he added.

Translated by Reinhold Grimm

Atlantis

Ein Land,
das es nie gab.

Aber es fällt
den Gedanken schwer,
es zu verlassen.

Helle Wege sind entstanden,
die zum Horizont führen.

Keine Müdigkeit.

Man muß die Dinge
nicht nur so sehen,
als seien sie schon gewesen.

Im Hafen
liegen die Schiffe,
die bei jeder Ausfahrt
das Meer hervorbringen.

Atlantis

A land
that never existed.

Yet our thoughts
find it hard
to abandon it.

Bright paths have emerged,
which lead toward the horizon.

No feeling of weariness.

One must consider things
not only as though
they had already been there.

Ships are
lying in harbor
that create the sea
whenever they leave port.

Translated by Reinhold Grimm

Labyrinth

Man kann darin weitergehen
und den Blick
auf die Dunkelheit einstellen.

Man kann die Wände abtasten,
um etwas zu tun.

Man kann rufen, auch wenn
man nicht weiß wozu.

Man kann sich verlieren,
sich finden.

Man kann also
darin leben.

Labyrinth

You can move on in it,
adjusting
your eyes to its darkness.

You can finger its walls
so as to do something.

You can shout, even though
you don't know what for.

You can lose yourself,
find yourself.

You can therefore
live in it.

Translated by Reinhold Grimm

Liebesgedicht (II)

Weil du die Tage
zu Schiffen machst,
die ihre Richtung kennen.

Weil dein Körper
lachen kann.

Weil dein Schweigen
Stufen hat.

Weil ein Jahr
die Form deines Gesichts annimmt.

Weil ich durch dich verstehe,
daß es Anwesenheit gibt,

liebe ich dich.

Love Poem (II)

Because you turn
the days into ships
that know their directions.

Because your body
is able to laugh.

Because your silence
has stages.

Because a year
takes on the shape of your face.

Because through you I understand
that presence does exist:

Therefore I love you.

Translated by Reinhold Grimm

Cyrus Atabay

Pallas

Granatapfel trägt die eine Hand,
die andere trägt den Helm,
die eine spendet Lethe,
die andere schwingt den Speer—:
halb nächtige du, halb helle.

Weiblich gestaltet, doch männlich kühn,
Goldene, die nie die Jungfräulichkeit verlor:
kaum in die Brautkammer geführte
und verschwundene schon—
kein Mann, kein Gott, der dich lange hielt.

Welches zweite Herz teilte deine Einsamkeit,
die ihren Schmerz bewahrt?
Kein Zeichen verrät die Herkunft
deiner Leichtigkeit,
die aus der Trauer stammt.

Das Gorgoangesicht ist auch das meine.
Verbündet mit dir nur im Tartaros,
bleibe ich nachtgebannt, indes du Lichte
die Höhle spaltest, dem Haupt entspringst,
weithinleuchtend vor die Götter trittst.

Gedenke dessen, der dir im Hades zugesellt,
wende dich um im Licht,
damit ihn dein Blick von fern her erreiche:
der blaue Schwalbenzug,
der seine Züge streift und die Schleier zerreißt.

Cyrus Atabay

Pallas

One of her hands holds a pomegranate,
the other one holds the helmet,
one dispenses lethe,
the other brandishes the spear—:
you, half nocturnal, half bright.

Of womanly shape, yet bold as a man,
golden one, who has never lost her virginity:
no sooner led to the bridal chamber
than vanished already—
no mortal, no god could retain you for long.

Where is a second heart to share your solitude
that keeps its pain?
No sign reveals the origin
of your gracefulness
deriving from grief.

The Gorgonian face is also mine.
Allied with you in Tartarus only, I
remain spellbound by its night, while you luminous one,
having cleft the cave, having sprung from the head,
step up to the gods in all your radiance.

Remember him, your companion in Hades,
turn around in the light
so that your gaze from afar may reach him:
the swallows' blue flock,
which touches his features and tears up the veils.

Translated by Reinhold Grimm

Peter Rühmkorf

Früher, als wir die großen Ströme noch

Früher, als wir die großen Ströme noch mit eigenen Armen teilten,
O b , L e n a , J e n i s s e i , M i s s o u r i ,
M i s s i s s i p p i , E l b e , O s t e ,
und mit Gesang den Hang raufzogen
und mit Gesang auch wieder herab,
immer den Augen hinterher und Hyperions leuchtenden Töchtern,
des Tages Anbruchs Röte
und des Mondes Aufzugs Beginn—
H e u t e : drei Telefongespräche und der Tag ist gelaufen.

Ja, man steht noch in Korrespondenz, das wohl . . .
Paar Gedankenstriche zu einer Ästhetik des Flickworts,
eine Hoffnung.
Etwas Zuspruch aus zahnlosen Mäulern,
ein Gewinn.
Dies nervöse Verflackern der fleißigen alten Kerle
kurz vorm Abschiednehmen,
ohne daß nochmal jemand richtig Reisig nachwirft—
Aber es ist immerhin nicht das erste Mal, daß du seufzt
und hoffentlich nicht das letzte,
irgendsoeine blindgeborene Mickymaus wird sich schon noch
        finden,
die deine Anlagen würdigt.

Peter Rühmkorf

Formerly, When We Still Parted the Big Rivers

Formerly, when we still parted the big rivers with our arms,
O b , L e n a , Y e n i s e y , M i s s o u r i ,
M i s s i s s i p p i , E l b e , O s t e ,
and, striking up songs, trooped up the slope
and, striking up songs, trooped down again,
always glued to our eyes and Hyperion's luminous daughters,
to the daybreak's red
and the beginning of the moon's procession—
N o w a d a y s: three telephone calls and the day is over.

Yeah, one still carries on a correspondence, to be sure . . .
Couple dashes for an aesthetic of the filler,
a hope.
Some comforting words out of toothless mugs,
a plus.
Those industrious old guys' nervous flickering out
shortly before their leave-taking,
without anyone soundly adding more brushwood to the fire—
But, after all, this isn't the first time you heave a sigh,
nor, let us hope, the last time;
some such blind-born Mickey Mouse will probably turn
        up,
that appreciates your talents.

Wenn man bedenkt, wie vielen trotzigen kleinen
Tante-Emma-Läden
du bis zum letzten Hirsekorn die Treue gehalten hast,
und sind ausnahmslos untergegangen . . .
Und dann kommt ja auch bald der Moment,
daß du selbst die Regale räumen mußt,
nur weil von hinten unentwegt die neue Ware nachdrückt:
Vom Dreck ergriffen steht die Menge da.
Nicht zur Hilfe eilen die Mitmenschen,
sondern zu niederen Schauzwecken.
Du aber sitzest angestrengt auf deinem Scherbenhügel
einen abgerissenen Fluch im Hals—

Alles Quack, wer der Welt zu tief ins Auge gesehn hat,
um noch an ihr leiden zu wollen,
wird den Mangel an Service hier nicht so persönlich nehmen.
Lieber als daß ich einiger abgesoffener Salatblätter wegen
gleich nach dem Chef des Hauses verlang,
laß ich mir doch das restliche Abendlicht auf der Netzhaut zergehn.
Ein paar dampfende Dachpfannen nach dem Regen.
Eine nasse Hecke, hingestreckt über tausend Meter,
eine Viertelstunde lang.
Ja, und am Ende sehnst du dich dann nach den Tagen,
die du jetzt so lieblos verabschiedest.

To think how many dogged little
corner stores
you've kept faith with until the very last millet grain,
they have gone under without exception . . .
And then, soon, there comes the moment, of course,
when you yourself must clear your racks,
only since, from behind, new goods are incessantly pressing:
Seized with that trash, the crowd is standing around.
Fellow humans don't rush to each other's assistance
but throng to the base rubbernecking.
You, though, you're sitting strenuously on your pile of shards,
with a cutoff curse in your throat—

All nonsense; whoever has looked the world too straight in the eye
to be willing to suffer from it any longer
won't take so personally the lack of service here.
Rather than asking at once to speak to the chef
just because of a few soaked and dripping salad leaves,
I do prefer to let the remaining evening light melt on my retina.
A couple of steaming pantiles after the rain.
A wet hedge, extending over a thousand meters,
a whole quarter hour.
Yeah, and in the end then you'll hanker after the days
that you now bid good-bye so unkindly.

Translated by Reinhold Grimm and Irmgard Hunt

Hans Magnus Enzensberger

Ins Lesebuch für die Oberstufe

Lies keine Oden, mein Sohn, lies die Fahrpläne:
sie sind genauer. Roll die Seekarten auf,
eh es zu spät ist. Sei wachsam, sing nicht.
Der Tag kommt, wo sie wieder Listen ans Tor
schlagen und malen den Neinsagern auf die Brust
Zinken. Lern unerkannt gehn, lern mehr als ich:
das Viertel wechseln, den Paß, das Gesicht.
Versteh dich auf den kleinen Verrat,
die tägliche schmutzige Rettung. Nützlich
sind die Enzykliken zum Feueranzünden,
die Manifeste: Butter einzuwickeln und Salz
für die Wehrlosen. Wut und Geduld sind nötig,
in die Lungen der Macht zu blasen
den feinen tödlichen Staub, gemahlen
von denen, die viel gelernt haben,
die genau sind, von dir.

Hans Magnus Enzensberger

For the Primer of Senior High

Don't read odes, son, read timetables:
they are more precise. Unroll the sea charts
before it is too late. Be watchful, don't sing.
The day will come when they will again nail to the door
blacklists, and brand the naysayers' chests
with marks of infamy. Learn how to move unrecognized,
learn more than I: to change the district, the passport,
the face. Know how to practice the petty betrayal,
the daily dirty escape. Useful indeed
are the encyclics to light a fire with,
the manifestoes to wrap up butter and salt
for the helpless. Fury and patience are needed
to blow into the lungs of power
the fine deadly dust, ground
by those who have learned much,
who are precise, by you.

Translated by Reinhold Grimm and Felix Pollak

Zum Andenken an William Carlos Williams

In seinem letzten Jahr war er fast blind,
heiter und sonderbar,
vertrat keine Ansichten, sah
nicht in die Röhre, las
keine Rezensionen,
weder *Look* noch *Life*.

Keine "repräsentative Figur":
Landarzt in Rutherford, New Jersey.
Keine Galadiners chez Kennedy:
eine Holzveranda,
"mit einem Blaugrün bemalt, das mir,
verwaschen, vergilbt, besser gefällt
als alle anderen Farben".

Für die Stockholmer Akademie
nicht ganz der Richtige,
für die Reporter unergiebig,
für *Look* nicht blind genug,
für *Life* zu lebendig
mit seinen achtzig Jahren,
sah er in seinem Hinterhof mehr
als ganz New York über zwölf Kanäle:

Hühner und kranke Leute,
das Licht und die Finsternis.

Nahm die Brille ab:
"Die Pflaumen im Eisschrank so süß und kalt" und
"Der Schritt des Alten, der Dünger sammelt,
ist majestätischer
als der von Hochwürden am Sonntag".

Sah die Finsternis und das Licht,
vergaß die Hühner nicht,
war genau
und sonderbar heiter.

In Memory of William Carlos Williams

In his last year, he was all but blind,
cheerful and peculiar,
expressed no opinions, didn't watch
the tube, didn't read
any reviews,
neither *Look* nor *Life*.

No "representative figure,"
country doctor in Rutherford, N.J.
No gala dinners *chez* Kennedy:
a wooden veranda,
"smeared a bluish green that,
weathered, faded, pleases me better
than all other colors."

For the Stockholm Academy
not quite right,
for the reporters unprofitable,
not blind enough for *Look,*
too alive for *Life*
with his eighty years
he perceived more in his backyard
than all of New York over twelve channels:

chickens and sick people,
the light and the darkness.

Took off his glasses:
"The plums in the icebox so sweet and cold" and
"The tread of the old man gathering dog-lime
is more majestic
than that of the Episcopal minister on Sunday."

Saw the darkness and the light,
did not forget the chickens,
was precise
and peculiarly cheerful.

Translated by Reinhold Grimm and Felix Pollak

Alte Revolution

Ein Käfer, der auf dem Rücken liegt.
Die alten Blutflecken sind noch da, im Museum.
Jahrzehnte, die sich totstellen.
Ein saurer Mundgeruch dringt aus dreißig Ministerien.
Im Hotel Nacional spielen vier verstorbene Musikanten
den Tango von 1959, Abend für Abend:
Quizás, quizás, quizás.

Im Gemurmel der tropischen Maiandacht
fallen der Geschichte die Augen zu.
Nur die Sehnsucht nach Zahnpasta,
Glühbirnen und Spaghetti
liegt schlaflos da zwischen feuchten Laken.

Ein Somnambule vor zehn Mikrophonen,
der kein Ende findet, schärft seiner müden Insel ein:
Nach mir kommt nichts mehr.
Es ist erreicht.
An den Maschinenpistolen glänzt das Öl.
Der Zucker klebt in den Hemden.
Die Prostata tut es nicht mehr.

Sehnsüchtig sucht der greise Krieger
den Horizont ab nach einem Angreifer.
Aber die Kimm ist leer. Auch der Feind
hat ihn vergessen.

Old Revolution

A beetle that lies on its back.
The old bloodstains are still there, in the museum.
Decades that pretend to be dead.
A sour bad breath is oozing from thirty ministries.
In the Hotel Nacional four deceased musicians
play the tango of 1959 every night:
Quizás, quizás, quizás.

In the murmur of the tropical May devotions
history can't keep its eyes open.
Only the nostalgia for toothpaste,
for light bulbs and spaghetti
is lying there, sleepless, between moist sheets.

A somnambulist in front of ten microphones,
unable to stop, impresses upon his weary island:
Nothing will come after me.
It is finished.
The oil on the tommy guns glistens.
The sugar sticks to the shirts.
The prostate gland won't work anymore.

With longing eyes, the aged warrior searches
the horizon for an aggressor.
But the dip is empty. The enemy, too,
has forgotten him.

Translated by Reinhold Grimm

Finnischer Tango

Was gestern abend war ist und ist nicht
Das kleine Boot das sich entfernt
und das kleine Boot das sich nähert
Das Haar das ganz nah war ist fremdes Haar
Das ist leicht gesagt Das ist immer so
Der graue See ist doch der graue See
Das frische Brot von gestern abend ist hart
Niemand tanzt Niemand flüstert Niemand weint
Der Rauch ist verschwunden und nicht verschwunden
Der graue See ist jetzt blau Jemand ruft
Jemand lacht Jemand ist fort
Es ist ganz hell Es war halb dunkel
Das kleine Boot kehrt nicht immer zurück
Es ist dasselbe und nicht dasselbe
Niemand ist da Der Felsen ist Felsen
Der Felsen hört auf Felsen zu sein
Der Felsen wird wieder zum Felsen
Das ist immer so Es verschwindet
nichts und nichts bleibt Was da war
ist und ist nicht und ist Das
versteht niemand Was gestern abend war
Das ist leicht gesagt Wie hell
der Sommer hier ist und wie kurz

Finnish Tango
In memory of Felix Pollak

That which existed last night is and isn't
The little boat that departs
and the little boat that approaches
The hair once so close is strange hair
That's easy to say   It's always like that
The gray lake is still the gray lake though
The new bread of last night is stale
No one dances No one whispers No one cries
The smoke has dissolved and yet hasn't
The gray lake is blue now   Someone calls
Someone laughs   Someone is gone
All is so bright   It was half dark
The little boat will not always return
It is the same and yet isn't
No one's around   The rock is a rock
The rock ceases being a rock
The rock turns into a rock again
It's always like that   Nothing
dissolves and nothing remains   What existed
is and isn't and is   No one
can grasp that   That which existed last night
That's easy to say   How bright
the summer here is and how brief

Translated by Reinhold Grimm

Der Krieg, wie

Er glitzert wie die zerbrochene Bierflasche in der Sonne
an der Bushaltestelle vor dem Altersheim

Er raschelt wie das Manuskript des Ghostwriters
auf der Friedenskonferenz

Er flackert wie der bläuliche Widerschein des Fernsehers
auf den somnambulen Gesichtern

Er riecht wie der Stahl der Maschinen im Fitness-Studio
wie der Atem des Leibwächters auf dem Flughafen

Er röhrt wie die Rede des Vorsitzenden
Er bläht sich wie die Fatwah im Munde des Ajatollah

Er zirpt wie das Videospiel auf der Diskette des Schülers
Er funkelt wie der Chip in Rechenzentrum der Bank

Er breitet sich aus wie die Lache hinter dem Schlachthof

Atmet
raschelt
bläht sich
riecht

wie

War, Like

It glitters like the smashed beer bottle in the sun
at the bus stop in front of the nursing home

It rustles like the ghostwriter's manuscript
at the peace conference

It flickers like the bluish reflection of the TV screen
on the somnambulistic faces

It smells like the steel of the fitness studio's machines
like the breath of the bodyguard at the airport

It bells like the speech of the chairman
It swells like the fatwah out of the mouth of the ayatollah

It chirps like the video game on the schoolboy's diskette
It glints like the chip at the bank's computing center

It spreads like the puddle behind the slaughterhouse

Breathing
rustling
it swells
smells

like

Translated by Reinhold Grimm

Die Reichen

Wo sie nur immer wieder herkommen,
diese üppigen Horden! Nach jedem Debakel
sind sie aus den Ruinen gekrochen,
ungerührt; durch jedes Nadelöhr
sind sie geschlüpft,
zahl-, stein- und segensreich.

Die Ärmsten. Niemand mag sie.
Schwer tragen sie an ihrer Last.
Sie beleidigen uns,
sind an allem schuld,
können nichts dafür,
müssen weg.

Wir haben alles versucht.
Gepredigt haben wir ihnen,
beschworen haben wir sie,
und erst als es nicht anders ging,
erpreßt, enteignet, geplündert.
Wir haben sie bluten lassen
und an die Wand gestellt.

Aber kaum ließen wir die Flinte sinken
und nahmen in ihren Sesseln Platz,
stellten wir fest, ungläubig
zuerst, dann aber aufatmend:
auch gegen uns war kein Kraut gewachsen.
Dochdoch, man gewöhnt sich an alles.
Bis zum nächsten Mal.

The Rich

From where on earth do they keep reemerging,
these luxuriant hordes! After every debacle
they come crawling out of the ruins,
unmoved; through the eyes of every needle
they have gone,
numer-, prosper-, felicitous.

Poor fellows. Nobody likes them.
Theirs is a burdensome lot.
They offend us,
it's all their fault,
they aren't to blame,
must go.

We've tried everything.
We preached to them,
we entreated them,
and only when there was no other way
did we blackmail, pillage, expropriate them.
We bled them,
formed firing squads and shot them.

Yet no sooner had we lowered our rifles
and taken our seats in their easy chairs
than we realized, disbelieving
at first, but then with a sigh of relief:
there was no remedy for us, either.
Suresure, one gets used to everything.
Until next time.

Translated by Reinhold Grimm

Zur Erinnerung an Sir Hiram Maxim (1840–1916)

1.

Auf dem Schulweg, im Straßengraben,
das Heulen des Tieffliegers, dann
Staubwölkchen links, vorne, rechts,
lautlos, und erst hinterher
das Hämmern der Bordkanone.
Die Bewunderung hielt sich in Grenzen.

2.

Später, viel später, taucht er auf
aus dem alten Lexikon. Ein Bauernjunge.
Die Farm in der Wildnis, heimgesucht
von den Bären. Das ist sehr lange her.
Mit vierzehn die Stellmacherlehre:
16 Stunden am Tag, vier Dollar Monatslohn.
Schlug sich durch als Gelbgießer,
Boxer, Instrumentenmacher, schrie:
Ein chronischer Erfinder bin ich!,
verbesserte Mausefallen, Lockenwickler
und baute ein pneumatisches Karussell.
Sein Dampfflugzeug, Kesselgewicht
1200 Pfund, drei Tonnen Speisewasser,
zerschellte am Eigengewicht.
Auch sein Kaffeersatz war kein Erfolg.
Erst die große Ausstellung in Paris,
eine Feerie aus Glühfäden und Bogenlampen,
brachte die Ehrenlegion und die Erleuchtung.

In Memory of Sir Hiram Maxim (1840–1916)

1.

On our way to school, in the ditch:
the strafer's roaring, then
small dust clouds, left, ahead, right,
soundless, and only thereafter
the clattering of the aircraft cannon.
Our admiration stayed within limits.

2.

Later, much later, he emerges
from the old encyclopedia. A country lad.
The farm in the wilderness, infested
with bears. That was a very long time ago.
At fourteen apprenticed to a cartwright:
16 hours a day, a monthly pay of four bucks.
Got along as a brass and bronze founder,
a boxer, an instrument maker, shouted:
A chronic inventor, that's what I am!,
improved on mousetraps, on curlers
and built a pneumatic merry-go-round.
His steam plane—the weight of its tank
1,200 pounds, with three tons of feed water—
crashed because of its dead load.
His ersatz coffee, too, was no success.
Only the great exhibition in Paris,
a fairy land of arc lamps and incandescent lights,
yielded the Legion of Honor as well as the illumination.

3.

Drei Jahre später konnte der Prince of Wales
in den Kellergängen von Hatton Garden
ein präzises Wunder besichtigen:
es lud, spannte, verriegelte, zog ab,
öffnete den Verschluß, warf die Hülse aus,
lud und spannte, immer wieder, von selbst,
und die Kadenz—fabelhaft! Die Kadenz:
zehn Schuß pro Sekunde, Dauerfeuer.
Der Rückstoßlader! Das ist genial,
rief der Duke of Cambridge, nie wieder
wird der Krieg sein, was er gewesen ist!
Eine Waffe von unerhörter Eleganz.
Der Ritterschlag folgte postwendend.

4.

Heute natürlich, wo diese Errungenschaft
auf jedem Schulhof zu haben ist,
fällt es schwer zu empfinden,
was er empfunden hat: die triebhafte Freude
eines bärtigen Säugetiers mit 270 Patenten.
Wir jedenfalls, hundert Jahre jünger als er,
lagen wie tot da am Straßenrand.

3.

Three years later the Prince of Wales
was privileged to inspect a precision miracle
in the underground hallways of Hatton Garden:
it loaded, cocked, locked, pulled the trigger,
opened the breechblock, ejected the cartridge case,
loaded and cocked, again and again, by itself,
and the cadence—fabulous! The cadence:
ten rounds per second, sustained fire.
The recoil-operated gun! That's ingenious,
exclaimed the Duke of Cambridge, never again
will war be what it has been before!
A weapon of unheard-of elegance.
The knighting followed posthaste.

4.

Nowadays, of course, when this great achievement
is available in every school yard,
it's difficult to feel
what he once felt: the instinctual delight
of a bearded mammal with 270 patents.
We, anyway, a hundred years younger than he,
were lying there by the roadside like dead.

Translated by Reinhold Grimm

Jürgen Becker

In der Nähe von Andy Warhol

als er dann wankte und umfiel,
der Schwarze auf dem Union Square,
hob ich ans Auge die Kamera
und sah im Sucher, daß
er liegen blieb
zwischen den gehenden Leuten.

Reiner Kunze

Die mauer
Zum 3. oktober 1990

Als wir sie schleiften, ahnten wir nicht,
wie hoch sie ist
in uns

Wir hatten uns gewöhnt
an ihren horizont

Und an die windstille

  In ihrem schatten warfen
alle keinen schatten

Nun stehen wir entblößt
jeder entschuldigung

Jürgen Becker

In the Proximity of Andy Warhol

as he then staggered and dropped to the ground,
that black man at Union Square,
I raised my camera to my eye
and perceived in its viewfinder that he
remained there lying
right between all those passers-by.

Translated by Reinhold Grimm

Reiner Kunze

The wall
For october 3, 1990

When we razed it, we didn't suspect
how high it still is
within us

We had accustomed ourselves
to its horizon

And to its dead calm

  In its shadow no one
ever cast a shadow

Now we are standing here
devoid of any excuse

Translated by Reinhold Grimm

Christoph Meckel

Rede vom Gedicht

Das Gedicht ist nicht der Ort, wo die Schönheit gepflegt wird.

Hier ist die Rede vom Salz, das brennt in den Wunden.
Hier ist die Rede vom Tod, von vergifteten Sprachen.
Von Vaterländern, die eisernen Schuhen gleichen.
Das Gedicht ist nicht der Ort, wo die Wahrheit verziert wird.

Hier ist die Rede vom Blut, das fließt aus den Wunden.
Vom Elend, vom Elend, vom Elend des Traums.
Von Verwüstung und Auswurf, von klapprigen Utopien.
Das Gedicht ist nicht der Ort, wo der Schmerz verheilt wird.

Hier ist die Rede von Zorn und Täuschung und Hunger
(die Stadien der Sättigung werden hier nicht besungen).
Hier ist die Rede von Fressen, Gefressenwerden
von Mühsal und Zweifel, hier ist die Chronik der Leiden.
Das Gedicht ist nicht der Ort, wo das Sterben begütigt
wo der Hunger gestillt, wo die Hoffnung verklärt wird.

Das Gedicht ist der Ort der zu Tode verwundeten Wahrheit.
Flügel! Flügel! Der Engel stürzt, die Federn
fliegen einzeln und blutig im Sturm der Geschichte!

Das Gedicht ist nicht der Ort, wo der Engel geschont wird.

Christoph Meckel

Speaking of the Poem

A poem is not the place where beauty is cherished.

We're speaking of salt that is burning in wounds.
We're speaking of death, of poisoned tongues.
Of fatherlands equalling iron boots.
A poem is not the place where truth is embellished.

We're speaking of blood that is flowing from wounds.
Of the misery, misery, misery of our dream.
Of devastation and scum, of shoddy utopias.
A poem is not the place where pain is forever healed.

We're speaking of wrath and deception and hunger
(stages of satiation are not being sung).
We're speaking here of devouring and being devoured,
of doubt and travail; this is the chronicle of suffering.
A poem is not the place where dying is soothed,
where hunger is appeased, and hope is transfigured.

A poem is the place of truth that is fatally wounded.
Wings! Wings! The angel crashes; his feathers,
torn off and bloody, are flying in History's tempest.

A poem is not the place where the angel is spared.

Translated by Reinhold Grimm

Sarah Kirsch

Die Luft riecht schon nach Schnee

Die Luft riecht schon nach Schnee, mein Geliebter
Trägt langes Haar, ach der Winter, der Winter der uns
Eng zusammenwirft steht vor der Tür, kommt
Mit dem Windhundgespann. Eisblumen
Streut er ans Fenster, die Kohlen glühen im Herd, und
Du Schönster Schneeweißer legst mir deinen Kopf in den
      Schoß
Ich sage das ist
Der Schlitten der nicht mehr hält, Schnee fällt uns
Mitten ins Herz, er glüht
Auf den Aschekübeln im Hof Darling flüstert die Amsel

Wintermusik

Bin einmal eine rote Füchsin ge-
Wesen mit hohen Sprüngen
Holte ich mir was ich wollte.

Grau bin ich jetzt grauer Regen.
Ich kam bis nach Grönland
In meinem Herzen.

An der Küste leuchtet ein Stein
Darauf steht: Keiner kehrt wieder.
Der Stein verkürzt mir das Leben.

Die vier Enden der Welt
Sind voller Leid. Liebe
Ist wie das Brechen des Rückgrats.

Sarah Kirsch

Already the Air Smells of Snow

Already the air smells of snow, my beloved
Wears his hair long, alas winter, that winter which
Throws us close together is almost upon us, comes on
With its team of greyhounds, scattering
Frostwork on the window. The coals are aglow in the hearth, and
You most beautiful one you snow-white one bury your head in
      my lap
I say that is
The sled which won't stop anymore; snow is falling
Into our very hearts, it glows
On the ash cans in the yard Darling whispers the blackbird

Translated by Reinhold Grimm

Winterly Music

I used to be, at one time, a red
Vixen with flying leaps
I fetched whatever I wanted.

Now I am gray a gray rain.
I got as far as Greenland
In my heart.

On the coast a rock is shining
Its message reads: Nobody will return.
That rock shortens my life.

The four ends of the earth
Are full of suffering. Love
Is like breaking one's own back.

Translated by Reinhold Grimm

Ich bin sehr sanft

Ich bin sehr sanft nenn
mich Kamille
meine Finger sind zärtlich baun
Kirchen in deiner Hand meine Nägel
Flügelschuppen von Engeln liebkosen ich bin
der Sommer der Herbst selbst der Winter im Frühling
möchte ich bei dir sein du
zeigst mir das Land wir gehn
von See zu See da braucht es
ein langes glückliches Leben
die Fische sind zwei
die Vögel baun Nester wir
stehn auf demselben Blatt

I Am Very Gentle

I am very gentle call
me camomile
my fingers are tender build
churches in your hands my fingernails
wingtips of angels caressing I am
summer autumn even winter in spring
I want to be for you You
show me the land we go
from lake to lake it takes
a long happy life
the fish are two
birds build nests it
is the same with us

Translated by Irmgard Hunt

Ich wollte meinen König töten

Ich wollte meinen König töten
Und wieder frei sein. Das Armband
Das er mir gab, den einen schönen Namen
Legte ich ab und warf die Worte
Weg die ich gemacht hatte: Vergleiche
Für seine Augen die Stimme die Zunge
Ich baute leergetrunkene Flaschen auf
Füllte Explosives ein—das sollte ihn
Für immer verjagen. Damit
Die Rebellion vollständig würde
Verschloß ich die Tür, ging
Unter Menschen, verbrüderte mich
In verschiedenen Häusern—doch
Die Freiheit wollte nicht groß werden
Das Ding Seele dies bourgeoise Stück
Verharrte nicht nur, wurde milder
Tanzte wenn ich den Kopf
An gegen Mauern rannte. Ich ging
Den Gerüchten nach im Land die
Gegen ihn sprachen, sammelte
Drei Bände Verfehlungen eine Mappe
Ungerechtigkeiten, selbst Lügen
Führte ich auf. Ganz zuletzt
Wollte ich ihn einfach verraten
Ich suchte ihn, den Plan zu vollenden
Küßte den andern, daß meinem
König nichts widerführe

I Wanted to Kill My King

I wanted to kill my king
And be free again. The bracelet
He gave me, the one beautiful name
I took off and threw the words
Away that I had made: metaphors
For his eyes, voice, and tongue
I stacked up empty bottles
Filled in explosives—that was to
Drive him away forever. To
Complete the rebellion
I locked the door, went
Among people, fraternized
In various houses—yet my
Freedom did not want to grow
The thing called soul that bourgeois thing
Not only persisted, became milder
Danced when I ran head-on
Against walls. I followed
The rumors abroad which
Spoke against him, collected
Three volumes of wrongdoing a file
Full of injustices, even lies
I listed. At the very end I
Just sought to betray him
I looked for him, to complete the plan
But kissed the other so that
Nothing should befall my king

Translated by Irmgard Hunt

Helga Novak

Brief an Medea

Medea du Schöne dreh dich nicht um
vierzig Talente hat er dafür erhalten
von der Stadt Korinth
der Lohnschreiber der
daß er dir den Kindermord unterjubelt
ich rede von Euripides verstehst du
seitdem jagen sie dich durch unsere Literaturen
als Mörderin Furie Ungeheuer
dabei hätte ich dich gut verstanden
wer nichts am Bein hat
kann besser laufen
aber ich sehe einfach nicht ein
daß eine schuldbeladene Gemeinde
ihre blutigen Hände an deinen Röcken abwischt
keine Angst wir machen
das noch publik
daß die Korinther selber deine zehn Gören gesteinigt haben
(wie sie schon immer mit Zahlen umgegangen sind)
und das mitten in Heras Tempel
Gewalt von oben hat keine Scham
na ja die Männer die Stadträte
machen hier so lustig weiter
wie früher und zu hellenischen Zeiten
(Sklaven haben wir übrigens auch)
bloß die Frauen kriegen neuerdings
Kinder auf Teufel komm raus
anstatt bei Verstand zu bleiben
(darin sind sie dir ähnlich)
andererseits haben wir
uns schon einigermaßen aufgerappelt
was ich dir noch erzählen wollte: die Callas ist tot

Helga Novak

Letter to Medea

Medea, you beautiful person, don't turn around
he received forty Talents for it
from the city of Corinth
the hack writer he
who pinned infanticide on you
I mean Euripides you know
since then they've chased you through literatures
as murderess fury and monster
and yet I would have understood you well
those who have nothing bound to their legs
can run better
but I just do not understand
how a guilt-ridden community
wipes off its bloody hands on your skirts
don't be afraid we'll make
it public yet
that the Corinthians themselves stoned your ten kids
(just like they always treat numbers)
and in the temple of Hera at that
official violence knows no shame
oh well the men of the town council
are carrying on jovially
just as before and in the Hellenic era
(we have slaves too by the way)
it's just that the women of late
are bearing children like mad
instead of keeping their wits about them
(in that they resemble you)
on the other hand we have
got back on our feet to a certain extent
another thing that I wanted to tell you: Callas is dead

Translated by S. L. Cocalis

Volker Braun

Wüstensturm

Saddam Hussein der lästige Lieferant
Dekoriert mit den Waffen seiner alten Kunden
NEBUKADNEZAR aus der Schule der Kolonien
In die Ecke der Welt gestellt
Der Norden lehrt den Süden Mores GOTT
MIT UNS / DIE MUTTER DER SCHLACHTEN
Der Schwelbrand der Hemisphären
Entflammt mit billigem Öl
Und Bagdad mein Dresden verlischt
OHNE GEWALT der Hoffnungsschrott des Herbstes
Die toten Soldaten des alten Jahrhunderts
Die Geisterheere im Endkampf des neuen.

Volker Braun

Desert Storm

Saddam Hussein the troublesome supplier
Decorated with weaponry of his long-standing patrons
NEBUCHADNEZZAR from the colonial school
Pushed into the corner of the world
The North is telling the South what's what GOD
WITH US / THE MOTHER OF ALL BATTLES
The smolder of the hemispheres
Kindled with inexpensive oil
And Baghdad my Dresden is fading away
WITHOUT VIOLENCE fall's scrap heap of hope
The dead soldiers of the old century
The phantom armies of the new one's Armageddon.

Translated by Reinhold Grimm

Rolf Dieter Brinkmann

Selbstbildnis im Supermarkt

für Dieter Wellershoff

In einer
großen
Fensterscheibe des Super-

markts komme ich mir selbst
entgegen, wie ich bin.

Der Schlag, der trifft, ist
nicht der erwartete Schlag
aber der Schlag trifft mich

trotzdem. Und ich geh weiter

bis ich vor einer kahlen
Wand steh und nicht weiter
weiß.

Dort holt mich später dann
sicher jemand

ab.

Rolf Dieter Brinkmann

Self-Portrait in the Supermarket

for Dieter Wellershoff

In a
big
windowpane of the super-

market I come to meet
myself, just as I am.

The blow that hits is
not the expected blow
but this blow hits me

nonetheless. And I keep going

till I stand before a bare
wall, at a loss how to keep on
going.

Yet later, someone will
surely pick me

up.

Translated by Reinhold Grimm

Irmgard Elsner Hunt

Mittag

Ich gehe mittags gern unter Bäumen
sie reichen herab verlangen nach mir halten
das Abwärtsgleiten des Tages in mir
auf suchen Verneinung und Trennung zu bannen
Buchen- und Lindengebärden ein Nicken
und Winken ein Rufen
im wiegenden Windatemrhythmus
ein einziges Wollen
ein Ja

auch könnte es sein ich begegnete ungeahnt dir
langsam und satt ins Blätterwerk blinzelnd
wir stünden und wüßten den Duft
ersten Sommerregens nach langer trockener Zeit zu
den dürstenden Gesten der Buchen und Linden zu tun
unsere Müdigkeit würde willens
den hohen Tag zu erneuern
uns und das Ja
zu verjüngen

Irmgard Elsner Hunt

Midday

I love to walk under trees at midday
they reach down, want to touch me, delay
the day from slipping away in-
side me, banish denial and parting
these gestures of beech and linden
are a nodding, a beck a call
in the sway of wind's breath, solely
desire
a yes

and perhaps unlooked for I would see you
peering passively, sated, into the foliage
we would stand there and know how to join
the sudden fragrance of first summer rain
to the thirsting gestures of beech and linden
our fatigue would eagerly renew
the peak of the day
rejuvenate us
and our yes

Translated by Sam McLean

Ursula Krechel

Früher November

Was ich vom Tag erwarte
die Dämmerung, die Nacht
die schon am Morgen lachte:
Erwarte mich.

Verstorbene Witwen zählen ihre Bestecke
ein Meckern an elektronischen Ladenkassen
ich doch vor Ihnen, aber bitte, Ursache keine.
Die Wolken spielen Sturmtheater
der Himmel bläht sich auf mit Plastiktüten
ich weine nicht, bin nicht alleine
der Tag verstreicht, verstrich, gestrichen
Äste bürsten den Horizont.

Ursula Krechel

Early November

What I expect from the day
is nothing but dusk, the night
that already laughed at dawn:
Expect but me.

Deceased widows are counting their cutlery
a nagging along electronic cash registers:
But I before you, oh please please, don't mention.
The clouds are staging a stormy show
the sky is blown up with plastic bags
I feel no woe, am not alone
the hours strike, have struck, are stricken.
Branches brush the horizon.

Translated by Reinhold Grimm

Nach Mainz!

Angela Davis, die Jungfrau Maria und ich
liegen in klammen weißen Betten
in einem Krankenhaus, dritte Klasse.
Wir reden nicht viel. Im Nebenraum
plärren die Säuglinge, die man uns abgepreßt hat.
Jede von uns ist an einem Wochentag
von einem gewöhnlichen Kind entbunden worden.
Maria liegt sehr blond in ihren Kissen.
Angela schläft viel. Ich lese in Freuds Traumdeutung
und frage mich, warum ich trotzdem
von pelzigen Säuge- und Nagetieren träume.
Pünktlich klopft eine Schwesternschülerin
und bringt die Düsseldorfer Nachrichten. Ausgerechnet
Düsseldorf, denke ich noch. Hier haben sie uns niedergestreckt.
Dann fällt mir die Schlagzeile auf: Zweite deutsche Teilung.
Alle Sozialisten nach Süddeutschland verbannt.
Demarkationslinie ist der Main.
Wir springen aus den Betten. Nichts wie nach Mainz
den Rhein hinauf. Wir umarmen uns, lachen
rennen barfuß durch die Altstadt zum Rhein.
Die Kinder, ruft Maria an einer roten Ampel.
Wir kehren nicht um. Die Nachkommen gehen eigene Wege.
Schon stehen wir bis zu den Knien in der grauen Brühe
bespritzen Brust und Arme und kraulen los.
Obwohl wir gegen den Strom schwimmen, kommen wir
gut voran. Was für ein Glück, die Arme auszustrecken
zu prusten, gurgeln, spritzen, um sich zu schlagen.
Hinter Wesseling ist das Wasser ganz klar.
Möwen begleiten uns eine Weile.
Während wir uns auf den Rücken werfen, reden wir
darüber, was uns erwartet. Ich kneife Angela in den Arm.
Wir träumen nicht. Am Loreleifelsen treffen wir
tatsächlich einen Fischer in seinem Nachen.
Er rudert gemächlich, damit er sich unterhalten kann.
Später bittet er uns in seinen Kahn.

To Mainz!

Angela Davis, the Virgin Mary, and I
are resting in dank white beds
in a hospital, third class.
We don't talk much. In the next room
the infants they have squeezed out of us cry.
Each of us delivered an ordinary child
on a weekday.
Mary is very blond on her pillows.
Angela sleeps a lot. I'm reading in Freud's dream
interpretations, asking myself why I nevertheless
dream of furry mammals and rodents.
Punctually the student nurse knocks
and brings the Düsseldorf paper. Of all places
Düsseldorf, I reflect. Here's where they grounded us.
Then I note the headlines: Second German Partition.
All Socialists Banished to South Germany.
Line of Demarcation Is the River Main.
We jump out of bed. We must get to Mainz fast
up the Rhine. We embrace and we laugh
and run barefoot through old town to the Rhine.
The children! cries Mary at a red light.
We don't turn back. The offspring will go its own way.
We are already knee-deep in the gray brine,
splash water on arms and chest, and are off, crawl-style.
Though we swim against current, we make
good progress. What bliss to stretch out our arms
to snort, gurgle, splash, and to flail about.
Past Wesseling the water is clear.
Seagulls escort us a while.
While turning on our backs, we talk about
what awaits us. I pinch Angela's arm.
We're not dreaming. At the Loreley cliff we actually
meet a fisherman in his boat.
He takes his time so that he can converse.
Later he invites us into his boat.

Besonders Maria weckt sein Interesse.
Sie gleiche einer bestimmten Person aufs Haar.
Manchmal schaut er ihr ins Gesicht. Bis nach Bingen
rudert er uns. Er zögert mitzukommen.
Einerseits sehe er unser historisches Glück
andererseits habe er Frau und Kinder.
Während wir ihm zuwinken, werden Boot und Mütze
kleiner und kleiner. Gegen Abend erreichen wir Mainz.
Von weitem schon sehen wir die Fahnen am Ufer.
Die Rote Hilfe begrüßt uns, reicht Decken
Frottiertücher. Wie mir die Knie zittern.

Friederike Roth

Ehe

Die Frau beschimpft ihn
und er sieht nur so aus dem Fenster.

Einmal war sie
ein schönes stilles Mädchen
schwarzweißes Wachsfräulein
mit feinen Armen, Händchen
die hielten ihn, den Kenner, fest.

Mary especially arouses his interest. Says he:
She resembles a certain someone to a tee.
Sometimes he looks into her face. Until Bingen
he rows us. He hesitates to come along. Says he:
On the one hand, he can see our historical moment
on the other, he has a wife and children.
While we wave to him, boat and cap become
smaller and smaller. Toward evening we reach Mainz.
From afar we see flags on the shoreline.
The Red Relief greets us, handing out blankets
and terrycloth towels. How my knees shake!

Translated by Irmgard Hunt

Friederike Roth

Marriage

The woman scolds him
but he just looks out the window.

Once she was
a beautiful quiet girl
black-and-white waxen maid
with fine arms, little hands
holding him, the connaisseur, fast.

Jetzt ist ein eignes Fest in ihren Augen
Erinnerungen von weit her:
        Großmutters Truhen geöffnet.
        Der Himmel
        lag auf den Hügeln vor der Tür.
        Und dahinein das Mädchen
        das einmal Brombeerpflücken ging.
        Und sie war dieses Mädchen.
        Was für ein Glück hätt' können sein
        wenn ein's gewesen wär.
Fort und fort
ein enthauptetes Leben
das wer verschuldet haben soll.

Er weiß von nichts.
So nimmt er's eben an
und seine Augen werden immer kleiner.

Fast Nacht um ihn.
Darin ist ausgestellt
feinsäuberlich der Herd, der Tisch, das Bett

gänzlich vermummt die Frau
und ohne Eingeweide
wie er selbst.

Er schließt die Augen.
In ihren liegen fremde Tränchen eh.

Now there's a peculiar hold in her eyes
remembrances as from far:
>   Grandmother's trunks, open.
>   The sky
>   lay on the hills outside the door.
>   And in this place the girl
>   who once went blackberry picking.
>   And she was that girl.
>   What happiness there could have been
>   if there had been any.
On and on
a life interdicted
of which someone is supposed to be guilty.

He knows of nothing.
So he just accepts it
and his eyes become smaller and smaller.

It's almost night around him.
In it arranged neatly
the stove, the table, the bed

quite muffled the woman
without intestines
like he himself.

He closes his eyes.
In hers lie strange tearlets ever.

Translated by Irmgard Hunt

Aus: "wiese und macht"

Lebendig bloß
atmend saugend am Anfang
ahnungsloses Gebrüll noch hinaus
hinein geschickt in die Welt:
Die weiß immer schon alles.
Läßt also den Dingen den Lauf
den sie ohnehin nehmen.

Untergehen wird
Hochstrebendes auferstehen
weltläufig und vertraut
aus Gelalle, Gebrüll
Zug um Zug eine Sprache
viel später
mitten im Sommer manchmal
fast immer im feuchten Moder im Herbst
manchmal erst ganz zum Schluß
Schweigen.
Ein Unversöhnliches. Ja.

From: "meadow and might"

Just only alive
breathing, sucking in the beginning
while still unsuspectingly screaming at it
discharged into the world:
She always knows everything already.
And so lets things take their course
as they will anyway.

The highly ambitious will go down
and rise again
ubiquitous and familiar
out of babbling, screaming
line for line a language
much later
in the middle of summer perhaps
almost always in the damp decay of fall
sometimes not until the very end
silence.
An irreconcilable one. Yes.

Translated by Irmgard Hunt

Holger Teschke

Bethlehemitischer Kindermord
(nach Brueghel)

Der Tanz der Stare über dem schlafenden Dorf
Seit zweitausend Jahren *Sie kommen immer am Morgen*
Würgengel in schimmernder Rüstung Stumm durch die Nacht
Verriegeln den Himmel schwarz mit Bannern und Lanzen
Zu Rama hat man ein Geschrei gehört Wer schreit
Rahel beweint ihre Kinder unterm Hundegebell
Selektiert nach Geschlecht und Alter *Was zweijährig ist und*
*   darunter*
Rahel will sich nicht trösten lassen von den Soldaten
Gib uns dein Kind Frau und wir machen dir ein neues
Für jeden Engel einen Bankert Komm ins Heu
Die Pferde zertrampeln den Schnee Kein Stern über Bethlehem
Die Heilige Nacht ist zu Ende Der Schlachttag geht seinen Gang

Dokumentarfilm

An den Tribünen vorbei des geliebten Führers
Atemlos jubelnd rennt das ergebene Volk
Die Hände erhoben Brüllend Wie auf der Flucht
Ein Schuh bleibt am Straßenrand liegen
        Ein Hut rollt aufs Pflaster
Im Kino das Publikum lacht Als wäre das alles
Ein Spuk aus Asien und nicht erst seit gestern vorbei
Und könnte nicht atemlos jubelnd wieder beginnen
Auf den Tribünen und Straßen der Stadt In dem Saal hier

Holger Teschke

The Massacre of the Innocents
(after Brueghel)

The dance of the starlings above the sleeping village
For two thousand years *They always come in the morning*
Destroying angels in shining armor Silently through the night
They bar the sky black with banners and lances
In Rama was there a lamentation heard Who laments
Rachel weeps to the barking of dogs for her children
Selected according to gender and age *Two years old and*
    under
Rachel would not be comforted by the soldiers
Give us your child woman and we'll get you pregnant again
For every angel a bastard Come to the haystack
The horses are stamping the snow No star above Bethlehem
The Holy Night is finished The day of slaughter is moving along

Translated by Reinhold Grimm

Documentary Film

Past the platforms of the beloved leader
The devoted people are running Breathlessly cheering
Hands raised Roaring As if taking flight
A shoe remains lying by the side of the street
    A hat rolls onto the pavement
In the movie theater the people are laughing As if all that
Were a nightmare from Asia and hadn't been over just yesterday
And couldn't begin again Breathlessly cheering
On the platforms and in the streets of the city Right in this room

Translated by Reinhold Grimm

Durs Grünbein

Pech für den zweiten Wurf

Zwei Uhr nachts, Zeit des Igels der
Bei den Mülltonnen stöbert
Während du zögernd
Wie auf Stacheln vorübergehst

Irgendwo in Europa, im selben
Mondflutlicht heimisch
Und wie dieser Igel
Raschelnd im Rinnstein

Irgendwo in Europa, nichtsahnend
Erfrischt von Novemberkälte
Und wie dieser Igel
Allzu mager für einen langen
Winterschlaf, allzu naiv

Sich nicht doch noch mit Äpfeln
Vollzustopfen um zwei Uhr nachts
Irgendwo in Europa
Und wie dieser Igel

Eine so leichte Beute der Zeit.

Durs Grünbein

Bad Luck with the Second Throw

2:00 A.M., time of the hedgehog that
   Roots round the garbage cans
      While you are passing
         Hesitantly, as if over spines

Somewhere in Europe, feeling at home in
   The same moony floodlight
      And just like this hedgehog
         Rustling around in the gutter

Somewhere in Europe, unsuspecting
   Refreshed by the chill of November
      And just like this hedgehog
         All too meager for an extended
         Hibernation, all too naive

For refraining from gorging yourself still
   With plenty of apples at 2:00 A.M.
      Somewhere in Europe
      And just like this hedgehog

Such an easy victim of time.

Translated by Reinhold Grimm

Alba

Endlich sind all die Wanderer tot
Und zur Ruhe gekommen die Lieder
Der Verstörten, der Landschaftskranken
In ihren langen Schatten, am Horizont.

Kleine Koseworte und Grausamkeiten
Treiben gelöst in der Luft. Wie immer
Sind die Sonnenbänke besetzt, lächeln
Kinder und Alte aneinander vorbei.

In den Zweigen hängen Erinnerungen,
Genaue Szenen aus einem künftigen Tag.
Überall Atem und Sprünge rückwärts
Durchs Dunkel von Urne zu Uterus.

Und das Neue, gefährlich und über Nacht
Ist es Welt geworden. So komm heraus
Aus zerwühlten Laken, sieh sie dir an,
Himmel, noch unbehelligt, und unten

Aus dem Hinterhalt aufgebrochen,
Giftige Gräser und Elstern im Staub,
Mit bösem Flügelschlag, Diebe
In der Mitte des Lebensweges wie du.

Alba

Finally, all the migrants are dead,
And to rest have come the songs of
The distracted, sick with landscapes
In their extended shadows, on the horizon.

Loving little pet names and cruelties
Float in the air, relaxed. As usual,
The sunny benches are occupied; children
And oldsters are smiling past one another.

In the branches, there dangle recollections,
Exact scenarios from a future day.
Everywhere breathing and leaping backward
Through the darkness from urn to uterus.

And new things, dangerously and overnight,
Have come into the world. So rise from
Your rumpled bedclothes, look at it all:
Skies, still undisturbed, and below them,

Having emerged from their ambuscades,
Toxic grasses and magpies in dust,
With an evil wingbeat, thieves
Midway through life, just like you.

Translated by Reinhold Grimm and Irmgard Hunt

Index of Authors

Index of Translators

Index of Titles or First Lines

Acknowledgments

Every reasonable effort has been made to locate the owners of rights to previously published works and the translations printed here. We gratefully acknowledge permission to reprint the following material:

Stefan George, *Sämtliche Werke* in 18 Bänden, Band VIII: *Der Stern des Bundes Klett-Cotta,* Stuttgart 1993.

Else Lasker-Schüller: "Mein blaues Klavier," Hugo von Hoffmannsthal: "Terzinen I: Über Vergänglichkeit," Gertrud Kolmar: "Das Einhorn," Bertolt Brecht: "Von armen B.B.," "An die Nachgeborenen," Marie Luise Kaschnitz: "Nicht mutig," "Vor der Tür," "Ein Gedicht," Peter Huchel: "[Ohne Titel]," "Rom," "Aristeas II," Günter Eich: "Inventur," "Wo ich wohne," "Der Mann in der blauen Jacke," "Ende eines Sommers," Karl Krolow: "Freier Fall," "Angst," "Robinson," "Der Wind im Zimmer," Paul Celan: "[Ohne Titel, EINMAL . . .]," "[Ohne Titel, NAH . . .]," "[Ohne Titel, DU . . .]," Hans Magnus Enzensberger: "Ins Lesebuch für die Oberstufe," "Zum Andenken an William Carlos Williams," "Alte Revolution," "Finnischer Tango," "Der Krieg, wie," "Die Reichen," "Zur Erinnerung an Sir Hiram Maxim," Ursula Krechel: "Früher November" reprinted by permission of Suhrkamp Verlag, Frankfurt am Main.

Ilse Aichinger — "Winterantwort" and "Briefwechsel," Johannes Bobrowski — "Osten" and "Trakl," Eugen Gomringer — "Worte," Ernst Jandl — "Im Delikatessenladen" and "Taschen," Else Lasker-Schüler — "Mein Volk/My People," Alfred Lichtenstein — "Der Morgen," Oskar Loerke — " Geleit," "Drunten" and "Berlin Winterabend," Ernst Meister — "Es war da ein anderes Haus," Nelly Sachs — "In der blauen Ferne" and "Der Schlafwandler," and Ernst Stadler — "Fahrt über die Kölner." In: *German Poetry 1910–1975: An Anthology.* Tr. and ed. by Michael Hamburger. © 1976 Urizen. Also printed by kind permission of Michael Hamburger.

Gottfried Benn, "Ein Wort /A Word." Tr. Richard Exner, reprinted by kind permission of the translator.

Franz Werfel — "Der Mensch ist Stumm" from *Gesammelte Werke. Das Lyrische Werk* — © 1967, Rose Ausländer — "Schlaffarben" from *Gesammelte Werke,* vol. 5, 1984, Hilde Domin — "Rückwanderung" from *Gesammelte Gedichte* 1987, Peter Huchel — "Chausseen" from *Chausseen Chausseen* © 1963. S. Fischer Verlag GmbH, Frankfurt am Main.

Hans Arp — "Kaspar ist tot / Kaspar Is dead," Georg Heym — "Umbra Vitae," Yvan Goll — "Reise ins Elend / Journey into Misery," Helmut Heissenbüttel — "Bruchstück III / Fragment III," in *Modern German Poetry 1910–1960.* Ed. Michael Hamburger and Christopher Middleton. New York: Grove Press, 1962. Also reprinted by kind permission of the translator Michael Hamburger.

Franz Werfel — "Das Bleibende" from *Gesammelte Werke: Das Lyrische Werk* © S. Fischer Verlag GmbH, Frankfurt am Main, 1967.

Yvan Goll, "In uralten Seen." All rights reserved by Wallstein Verlag, Göttingen.

Elisabeth Langgässer: "Gedichte" © 1959 Claassen Verlag.

Marie Luise Kaschnitz — "Hiroshima" from *Selected Later Poems of Marie Luise Kaschnitz,* Copyright © 1980 by Princeton University Press.

Günter Eich, "Inventory" and "Where I Live," in *Valuable Nail,* FIELD Translation Series 5, trans. by Stuart Friebert, David Walker, and David Young, Oberlin: Oberlin College Press, ©1981. Reprinted by permission of Oberlin College Press.

Hilde Domin, "Rückwanderung." In: *Four German Poets: Günter Eich, Hilde Domin, Erich Fried, Günter Kunert.* Tr. Agnes Stein. Copyright © 1979. Erich Fried, "Invitation to Forget" and "Retrospect." In: *100 Poems without a Country.* Tr. Stuart Hood. Copyright © 1980. Red Dust, New York.

Johannes Bobrowski, *Gesammelte Werke, Band I: Die Gedichte.* Copyright © 1998. Sarah Kirsch — "Die Luft riecht schon nach Schnee," "Ich bin sehr sanft," "Wintermusik," and "Ich wollte meinen König töten." Copyright © Sarah Kirsch, *Werke in Jong Bänden* 1999. Deutsche Verlags-Anstalt GmbH, Stuttgart.

Paul Celan, "Psalm," taken from: *Die Niemandsrose.* © S. Fischer Verlag, Frankfurt am Main, 1963.

Erich Fried — "Logos." In: *Gesammelte Werke: Gedichte I.* Berlin: Wagenbach, 1993. Marie Luise Kaschnitz — "Hiroshima." Printed with the permission of Econ Ullstein List Verlag GmbH & Co. KG.

Erich Fried — "Einbürgerung" aus *und Vietnam und.* © 1966. Erich Fried — "Aufforderung zum Vergessen" aus *100 Gedichte ohne Vaterland.* © 1978. Erich Fried — "Rückblick" aus *Die bunten Getüme.* © 1977. Verlag Klaus Wagenbach, Berlin.

Walter Höllerer — "Verweile einen Atemzug, unstetes Tier" and "Der lag besonders mühelos am Rand" printed by kind permission of the author.

Margot Scharpenberg — "Rotes Tulpenfeld." In: *Margot Scharpenberg: Wenn Farben blühen.* Mühlacker: Stieglitz Verlag 1999. Also printed by kind permission of the author.

Ingeborg Bachmann — "Alle Tage," "Nebelland," "Das erstgeborene Land," "Wahrlich" printed by permission of Piper Verlag GmbH. © Piper Verlag GmbH, München, 1978. "An die Sonne." In: *Werke.* Ed. Christine Koschel et al. Munich: Piper, 1978. Also by kind permission of the heirs of Ingeborg Bachmann.

Günter Grass — "Wandlung" and "Danach." In: *Gedichte und Kurzprosa.* Werkausgabe, Band I. Copyright © Steidl Verlag, Göttingen 1997

Günter Kunert, "Verlorenes Venedig" and "Der jüdische Friedhof in Weißensee" in: *Berlin Beizeiten: Gedichte,* 1987, Copyright © 1987. "Theatrum mundi" in: *Abtötungsverfahren: Gedichte,* 1980, Copyright © 1980. Carl Hanser Verlag München, Wien. Also by permission of the author, Günter Kunert. "Sestri Levante (Ligurien II)" reprinted by kind permission of the author.

Walter Helmut Fritz: "Fast verschämt." Aus: *Das offene Fenster. Prosagedichte.* Copyright © 1997. Walter Helmut Fritz: "Das Fiasko." Aus: *Die Schlüssel sind vertauscht. Gedichte und Prosagedichte 1987–1991.* Copyright © 1992. "Columbus," "Labyrinth" und "Liebesgedicht." Aus: *Die Zuverlässigkeit der Unruhe. Neue Gedichte.* Copyright © 1966 Walter Helmut Fritz: "Atlantis." Aus: *Schwierige Überfahrt. Gedichte.* Copyright © 1976 by Hoffmann und Campe Verlag, Hamburg.

Cyrus Atabay, "Pallas." In: *An- Und Abflüge: Gedichte,* 1958. © 1958 Carl Hanser Verlag München, Wien.

Helga Novak (1935–), "Letter to Medea" *(Brief an Medea),* and Ursula Krechel (1947–), "To Mainz!" *(Nach Mainz!).* English translations by S. L. Cocalis. Reprinted by permission of The Feminist Press at The City University of New York, from *The Defiant Muse: German Feminist Poems from the Middle Ages to the Present, A Bilingual Anthology,* edited by Susan L. Cocalis. Translation copyright © 1986 by S. L. Cocalis. Compilation copyright © 1986 by Susan L. Cocalis.

Volker Braun — "Wüstensturm" reprinted by kind permission of the author.

Holger Teschke, "Dokumentarfilm," In: *H. T., Jasmunder Felder Windschlucht New York. Gedichte* © Aufbau-Verlag Berlin und Weimar, 1991.

Holger Teschke — "Bethlehemitischer Kindermord (nach Breughel)." In: *Gedichte und Interpretationen Band 7: Gegenwart II.* Hg. Walter Hinck. Reclam, 1997. Also reprinted by kind permission of the author.

Titles Available in The German Library

All titles available from Continuum International
370 Lexington Avenue, New York, NY 10017
www.continuumbooks.com

Titles Available in The German Library

Eschenbach, Luther, Gryphius,
and Others
GERMAN POETRY FROM THE
BEGINNINGS TO 1750

Eighteenth Century

Volume 10
Heinse, La Roche, Wieland, and
Others
EIGHTEENTH CENTURY GERMAN
PROSE

Volume 11
Herder, Lenz, Lessing, and Others
EIGHTEENTH CENTURY GERMAN
CRITICISM

Volume 12
Gotthold Ephraim Lessing
NATHAN THE WISE, MINNA VON
BARNHELM, AND OTHER PLAYS AND
WRITINGS

Volume 13
Immanuel Kant
PHILOSOPHICAL WRITINGS

Volume 14
Lenz, Heinrich Wagner, Klinger,
and Schiller
STURM UND DRANG

Volume 15
Friedrich Schiller
PLAYS: INTRIGUE AND LOVE, AND
DON CARLOS

Volume 16
Friedrich Schiller
WALLENSTEIN AND MARY STUART

Volume 17
Friedrich Schiller

ESSAYS: LETTERS ON THE AESTHETIC
EDUCATION OF MAN, ON NAIVE
AND SENTIMENTAL POETRY, AND
OTHERS

Volume 18
Johann Wolfgang von Goethe
FAUST PARTS ONE AND TWO

Volume 19
Johann Wolfgang von Goethe
THE SUFFERINGS OF YOUNG
WERTHER AND ELECTIVE AFFINITIES

Volume 20
Johann Wolfgang von Goethe
PLAYS: EGMONT, IPHIGENIA IN
TAURIS, TORQUATO TASSO

Nineteenth Century

Volume 21
Novalis, Schlegel, Schleiermacher,
and Others
GERMAN ROMANTIC CRITICISM

Volume 22
Friedrich Hölderlin
HYPERION AND SELECTED POEMS

Volume 23
Fichte, Jacobi, and Schelling
PHILOSOPHY OF GERMAN IDEALISM

Volume 24
Georg Wilhelm Friedrich Hegel
ENCYCLOPEDIA OF THE
PHILOSOPHICAL SCIENCES IN
OUTLINE AND CRITICAL WRITINGS

Volume 25
Heinrich von Kleist
PLAYS: THE BROKEN PITCHER,
AMPHITRYON, AND OTHERS

Titles Available in The German Library

Titles Available in The German Library

Titles Available in The German Library

Titles Available in The German Library

Complete Author Listing
in The German Library
by Volume Number